Hands-On Entity Resolution

A Practical Guide to Data Matching
with Python

Michael Shearer

Beijing · Boston · Farnham · Sebastopol · Tokyo

Hands-On Entity Resolution

by Michael Shearer

Published by O'Reilly Media, Inc., 1005 Gravenstein Highway North, Sebastopol, CA 95472.

O'Reilly books may be purchased for educational, business, or sales promotional use. Online editions are also available for most titles (*https://oreilly.com*). For more information, contact our corporate/institutional sales department: 800-998-9938 or *corporate@oreilly.com*.

Acquisitions Editor: Michelle Smith	**Indexer:** Judith McConville
Development Editor: Jeff Bleiel	**Interior Designer:** David Futato
Production Editor: Kristen Brown	**Cover Designer:** Karen Montgomery
Copyeditor: Stephanie English	**Illustrator:** Kate Dullea
Proofreader: Krsta Technology Solutions	

February 2024:   First Edition

Revision History for the First Edition

2024-02-01:   First Release

See *https://oreilly.com/catalog/errata.csp?isbn=9781098148485* for release details.

978-1-098-14848-5

[LSI]

Table of Contents

Preface

We all want to make better decisions. Whether it's to better serve our customers or to keep them safe, we want to make the right judgments and do the right thing. To act with confidence we need to understand who we are serving and what their place is in the world. While there is often an avalanche of data available to us, too often it isn't joined up and doesn't tell us the full story of the individual before us.

Entity resolution is the art and science of connecting the data, joining the dots, and seeing the full picture. This book is a practical guide to help you reveal that wider context and help you be fully informed before you act. It's often taken for granted, but you'll see in this book that matching up data isn't always straightforward—but don't worry, by the final chapter you'll be well equipped to overcome these challenges and bring your datasets to life.

Who Should Read This Book

If you are a product manager, a data analyst, or a data scientist within financial services, pharmaceuticals, or another large corporation, this book is for you. If you are struggling with the challenges of siloed data that doesn't join up, have competing views of your customers in different databases, or are charged with merging information from different organizations or affiliates, this book is for you.

Risk management professionals charged with combating financial crime and managing reputation and supply chain risks will also benefit from understanding the data matching challenges laid out in this book and the techniques to overcome them.

Why I Wrote This Book

The challenge of entity resolution is all around us—we may not use those words but every day this process is repeated time and again. A few weeks before completion of this book, my wife asked me to help her check names off a list as she read out a list of payers from a bank statement. Had all the people on the list paid? This was entity resolution in action!

The idea for this book was born out of a desire to explain why checking for a match against a list of names is not as easy as it sounds, and to showcase some of the amazing tools and techniques that are now available to help solve this problem at scale.

I hope that by guiding you through some real-life examples you will feel confident in matching up your datasets so that you can serve and protect your customers. I'd love to hear about your journey and any feedback on the book itself. Please feel free to raise any issues with code that accompanies this book on GitHub (*https://github.com/mshearer0/HandsOnEntityResolution*), or to discuss entity resolution in general, please contact me on LinkedIn (*https://www.linkedin.com/in/mshearer0*).

Entity resolution is an art, as well as a science. There is no one-size-fits-all prescribed solution that will work for every dataset. You will need to make decisions about how to tune your process to achieve the results you want. I hope that readers of this book will be able to help each other find the optimum solutions and benefit from shared experiences.

Navigating This Book

This book is intended as a hands-on guide, so I encourage you to follow along with the code as you work through each chapter. A key design tenet of the book was to illustrate the challenges and solutions using real-world open source data. This brings with it some challenges if you are following along because your results may vary slightly as the source dataset is updated from the date of publication. Please check the GitHub page (*https://github.com/mshearer0/HandsOnEntityResolution*) for any recent updates and to access the code that accompanies the book.

- Chapter 1 provides a basic introduction to entity resolution, why it is needed, and the logical steps in the process.
- Chapter 2 illustrates the importance of standardizing and cleansing data before attempting to match records together.
- Chapters 3 through 6 show how to compare data records to resolve entities using approximate comparisons and probabilistic matching techniques.

- Chapter 7 describes the process of grouping together records describing the same entity into a uniquely identifiable cluster.

- Chapters 8 and 9 illustrate how to scale up the entity resolution process using cloud computing services.

- Chapter 10 shows how records can be linked while preserving privacy between data owners.

- Finally, Chapter 11 describes some further considerations when designing an entity resolution process and offers a few closing thoughts on likely future developments.

I would recommend Chapters 2 through 9 be read consecutively because they incrementally build entity resolution solutions using shared problem datasets.

This book assumes a basic understanding of Python. Interactive tutorials are available at *http://learnpython.org* to get started, or I recommend *Python for Data Analysis* by Wes McKinney (O'Reilly). More advanced readers would benefit from knowledge of pandas, Spark, and Google Cloud Platform.

Conventions Used in This Book

The following typographical conventions are used in this book:

Italic
> Indicates new terms, URLs, email addresses, filenames, and file extensions.

`Constant width`
> Used for program listings, as well as within paragraphs to refer to program elements such as variable or function names, databases, data types, environment variables, statements, and keywords.

`Constant width bold`
> Shows commands or other text that should be typed literally by the user.

`Constant width italic`
> Shows text that should be replaced with user-supplied values or by values determined by context.

> This element signifies a general note.

This element indicates a warning or caution.

Using Code Examples

Supplemental material (code examples, exercises, etc.) is available for download at *https://github.com/mshearer0/HandsOnEntityResolution*.

If you have a technical question or a problem using the code examples, please send email to *support@oreilly.com*.

This book is here to help you get your job done. In general, if example code is offered with this book, you may use it in your programs and documentation. You do not need to contact us for permission unless you're reproducing a significant portion of the code. For example, writing a program that uses several chunks of code from this book does not require permission. Selling or distributing examples from O'Reilly books does require permission. Answering a question by citing this book and quoting example code does not require permission. Incorporating a significant amount of example code from this book into your product's documentation does require permission.

We appreciate, but generally do not require, attribution. An attribution usually includes the title, author, publisher, and ISBN. For example: "*Hands-On Entity Resolution* by Michael Shearer (O'Reilly). Copyright 2024 Michael Shearer, 978-1-098-14848-5."

If you feel your use of code examples falls outside fair use or the permission given above, feel free to contact us at *permissions@oreilly.com*.

O'Reilly Online Learning

O'REILLY® For more than 40 years, *O'Reilly Media* has provided technology and business training, knowledge, and insight to help companies succeed.

Our unique network of experts and innovators share their knowledge and expertise through books, articles, and our online learning platform. O'Reilly's online learning platform gives you on-demand access to live training courses, in-depth learning paths, interactive coding environments, and a vast collection of text and video from O'Reilly and 200+ other publishers. For more information, visit *https://oreilly.com*.

How to Contact Us

Please address comments and questions concerning this book to the publisher:

O'Reilly Media, Inc.
1005 Gravenstein Highway North
Sebastopol, CA 95472
800-889-8969 (In the United States or Canada)
707-827-7019 (international or local)
707-829-0104 (fax)
support@oreilly.com
https://www.oreilly.com/about/contact.html

We have a web page for this book, where we list errata, examples, and any additional information. You can access this page at *https://oreil.ly/handsOnEntityResolution*.

For news and information about our books and courses, visit *https://oreilly.com*.

Find us on LinkedIn: *https://linkedin.com/company/oreilly-media*.

Follow us on Twitter: *https://twitter.com/oreillymedia*.

Watch us on YouTube: *https://youtube.com/oreillymedia*.

Acknowledgments

I have learned that writing a book is very much a team effort. I am grateful to have been given the time and space to assemble this guide and for everyone who said yes, and gave their time freely, to make it happen.

First, I'd like to acknowledge Aurélien Géron, whose book *Hands-On Machine Learning with Scikit-Learn, Keras, and TensorFlow* inspired me to consider writing a hands-on guide. I'd also like to express my appreciation to all my former colleagues at HSBC who put entity resolution techniques to such good use in combatting financial crime.

I'd like to thank everyone at O'Reilly, starting with Michelle Smith, Senior Content Acquisitions Editor, for entertaining the initial idea and crafting the proposal. Sincerest thanks to Jeff Bleiel for his editorial skill and guiding hand throughout the drafting process. Thanks to Aleeya Rahman, Production Editor, for her guidance on formatting and the art of LaTeX, and to Kristen Brown, Manager, Content Services, for publishing the early releases, which were such an encouraging milestone. I'd also like to recognize Karen Montgomery for such a fitting front cover illustration—are the birds a match?

I am especially grateful to reviewers Robin Linacre, Olivier Binette, and Juan Amador. Thanks to Juan for introducing me to the topic of entity resolution several years ago and inspiring me to learn more; to Olivier for his expert guidance on the state-of-the-art and his pioneering work on evaluation; and to Robin for his commitment to explaining the complexities of entity resolution in a practical, accessible way. I'd also like to acknowledge the Splink and OpenMined teams for the open source frameworks upon which much of this book is based—"standing on the shoulders of giants" comes to mind.

Lastly, I'd like to pay tribute to my beloved wife, Kay, for her support and patience throughout the process. I'd also like to thank my daughters: Abigail for challenging me to frame the subject in an accessible way and Emily for encouraging me to never give up!

CHAPTER 1

Introduction to Entity Resolution

All around the world vast quantities of data are being collected and stored, and more data is being added every day. This data records the world we live in and the changing attributes and characteristics of the people, places, and things around us.

Within this global ecosystem of data processing, organizations independently collect overlapping sets of information about the same real-world entity. And each organization has its own approach to organizing and cataloging the data it holds.

Companies and institutions seek to derive valuable insights from this raw data. Advanced analytical techniques have been developed to discern patterns in the data, extract meaning, and even attempt to predict the future. The performance of these algorithms depends on the quality and richness of the data fed into them. By combining data from more than one organization, often a richer, more complete dataset can be created, from which more valuable conclusions can be drawn.

This book will guide you through how to join these heterogeneous datasets to create richer sets of data about the world in which we live. This process of joining datasets is known by a variety of names including name matching, fuzzy matching, record linking, entity reconciliation, and entity resolution. In this book we will use the term *entity resolution* to describe the overall process of resolving, that is, joining, data together that refers to real-world entities.

What Is Entity Resolution?

Entity resolution is a key analytic technique to identify data records that refer to the same real-world entity. This matching process enables the removal of duplicate entries within a single source and the joining of disparate data sources when common unique identifiers are not available.

Entity resolution enables enterprises to build rich and comprehensive data assets, to reveal relationships, and to construct networks for marketing and risk management purposes. It is often a key prerequisite to harness the full potential of machine learning and AI.

For example, healthcare providers often need to join records from across different practices or historical archives held on different platforms. In financial services, customer databases need to be reconciled to offer the most relevant products and services or to enable fraud detection. To enhance resilience or provide transparency on environmental and social issues, corporations need to join supply chain records with sources of risk intelligence.

Why Is Entity Resolution Needed?

In everyday life as individuals, we are assigned a lot of numbers—according to my healthcare provider, I am identified by one number, another by my employer, another by my national government, and so on. When I sign up for services, I'm often assigned a number (or more than one sometimes) by my bank, chosen retailer, or online provider. Why all these numbers? Back in a simpler time, when services were delivered in a local community, customers were known personally and interactions were conducted face to face, it was obvious who you were dealing with. Exchanges were often discrete transactions with no need to refer to any prior business and no need to keep records associated with individual customers.

As more and more services began to be provided remotely and offered on a wider regional or even national basis, a means of identifying who was who became necessary. Names were clearly insufficiently unique, so names were often combined with location to create a composite identifier: Mrs. Jones became Mrs. Jones from Bromley as opposed to Mrs. Jones from Harrow. As records migrated from paper to electronic form, the assignment of a unique machine-readable number began the era of numeric, and alphanumeric, identifiers that surround us today.

Within the confines of their own domain these identifiers usually work well. I identify myself with my unique number and it's clear that I'm the same returning individual. This identifier allows a common context to be quickly established between two parties and reduces the possibility of misunderstanding. These identifiers typically have nothing in common, vary in length and format, and are assigned according to different schemes. There is no mechanism to translate between them or to identify that individually and collectively they refer to me and not another individual.

However, when business is depersonalized, and I don't know the person I'm dealing with and they don't know me, what happens if I register for the same service more than once? Perhaps I've forgotten to identify with my unique number or a new application is being submitted on my behalf. A second number will be created that also identifies me. This duplication makes it more difficult for the service provider to offer a personalized service as they must now join together two different records to understand fully who I am and what my needs might be.

Within larger organizations, the problem of matching up customer records becomes even more challenging. Different functions or business lines may maintain their own records that are specifically tailored to their purpose but were designed independently of each other. A common problem is how to construct a comprehensive (or 360 degree) view of a customer. Customers may have interacted with different parts of an organization over many years. They may have done so in different contexts—as an individual, as part of a joint household, or perhaps in an official capacity associated with a company or other legal entity. In the course of these different interactions, the same person may have been assigned a multiplicity of identifiers in various systems.

This situation commonly arises due to (often historic) mergers and acquisitions, where overlapping sets of customers are to be amalgamated and treated consistently as a single population. How do we match up a customer from one domain with one from another?

This challenge of joining records also occurs when bringing together datasets supplied by different organizations. Because there is typically no universally adopted standard or common key between enterprises, especially with respect to individuals, the joining of their data is a commonly overlooked and nontrivial exercise.

Main Challenges of Entity Resolution

If our assigned unique identifiers are all different and don't match up, how can we identify that two records refer to the same entity? Our best approach is to compare individual attributes of those entities, such as their name, and if they share enough similarities, make our best judgment that they are a match. This sounds simple enough, right? Let's delve into some of the reasons why that isn't as straightforward as it sounds.

Lack of Unique Names

First, there is the challenge of recognizing uniqueness between names or labels. The repeated assignment of the same name to different real-world entities presents an obvious challenge in differentiating who is who. Perhaps you searched the internet for your own name. Chances are, unless your name is particularly uncommon, you will have found plenty of doppelgangers with exactly the same name as yourself.

Inconsistent Naming Conventions

Names are recorded in a variety of ways and data structures. Sometimes names are described in full, but often abbreviations are present or less significant parts of the name are omitted. For example, my name might be expressed, entirely correctly, as any of the variations in Table 1-1.

Table 1-1. Name variations

Name
Michael Shearer
Michael William Shearer
Michael William Robert Shearer
Michael W R Shearer
M W R Shearer
M W Shearer

None of these names exactly match each other but all refer to the same person, the same real-world entity. Titles, nicknames, shortened forms, or accented characters all frustrate the process of finding an exact match. Double-barreled or hyphenated last names add further permutations.

In an international context, naming practices vary enormously across the globe. Personal names may be present at the start or the end of a name and family names may or may not be present. Family names may also vary according to the sex and marital status of the individual. Names may be written in a variety of alphabets/character sets or translated differently between languages.[1]

Data Capture Inconsistencies

The process of capturing and recording names or labels usually reflects the data standards of the acquirer. At the most basic level, some data acquisition processes will employ uppercase characters only, others lowercase, while many will permit mixed case with initial letters capitalized.

A name may be heard only in conversation without the opportunity to clarify the correct spelling or may be incorrectly transcribed in a hurry. Names or labels are often mistyped during manual rekeying or accidentally omitted. Sometimes different conventions are used that can easily be interpreted incorrectly if the original context is lost. For example, even a simple name can be recorded as "First name, Last name," or perhaps as "Last name, First name," or even transposed completely into the wrong fields.

International data capture can lead to inconsistencies in transliteration between one script and another, or to transcription errors when captured verbally.

---

1 For further details on global naming conventions, see this guide (*https://oreil.ly/Hzu6D*).

Worked Example

Let's consider a simple fictitious example to illustrate how these challenges might manifest themselves. To begin with, imagine the only information we have is the name, as shown in Table 1-2.

Table 1-2. Example records

Name
Michael Shearer
Micheal William Shearer

Is it likely that a "Michael Shearer" refers to the same entity as a "Micheal William Shearer"? Absent any other information, there is a fair chance that both refer to the same person. The second, with the addition of a middle name, has extra information but otherwise they are nearly identical and a comparison of the two last names would produce an exact match. Notice I slipped in a common misspelling of my first name. Did you spot it?

What if we add another attribute—can that help improve our matching accuracy? If you can't remember your membership number, a service provider will often ask for a date of birth to help identify you (they also do this for security reasons). Date of birth is a particularly helpful attribute because it doesn't change and has a large number of potential values (known as *high cardinality*). Also, the composite structure of individual values for day, month, and year may give us clues to the likelihood of a match when an exact equivalence isn't established. For example, consider Table 1-3.

Table 1-3. Example records—2

Name	Date of birth
Michael Shearer	1/4/1970
Micheal William Shearer	14 January 1970

At first glance the date of birth is not equivalent between the two records, so we might be tempted to discount the match. If these two individuals are born 10 days apart, they are unlikely to be the same person! However, there is only a single-digit difference between the two, with the former lacking the leading digit 1 in the day subfield—could this be a typo? It's hard to tell. If the records were from different sources, we would also have to consider whether the data format was consistent—do we have the UK format of DD/MM/YYYY or the US format of MM/DD/YYYY?

What if we add a place of birth? Again, this attribute shouldn't change but it can be expressed at different levels of granularity or with different punctuation. Table 1-4 shows the enriched records.

Table 1-4. Example records—3

Name	Date of birth	Place of birth
Michael Shearer	1/4/1970	Stow-on-the-Wold
Micheal William Shearer	14 January 1970	Stow on the Wold

Here there is no exact match on the place of birth between either record, although both could be factually correct.

Therefore, place of birth, which may be recorded at different levels of specificity, doesn't help us as much as we thought it might. What about something more personal, like a phone number? Of course, many of us do change our phone number throughout our life but with the ability to keep a cherished and well socialized mobile phone number when swapping between providers, this number is a more sticky attribute that we can use. However, even here we have challenges. Individuals may possess more than one number (a work and a personal number, for example), or the identifier may be recorded in a variety of formats, including spaces or hyphens. It may include or exclude an international dialing prefix.

Table 1-5 shows our complete records.

Table 1-5. Example records—4

Name	Date of birth	Place of birth	Mobile number
Michael Shearer	1/4/1970	Stow-on-the-Wold	07700 900999
Micheal William Shearer	14 January 1970	Stow on the Wold	0770-090-0999

As you can see, this resolution challenge is quickly becoming quite complicated.

Deliberate Obfuscation

The vast majority of data inconsistencies that frustrate the matching process arise through inattentive but well-meaning data capture processes. However, for some uses we must consider the scenario where data has been maliciously obfuscated to disguise the true identity of the entity and prevent associations that might reveal a criminal intent or association.

Match Permutations

If I asked you to match your name against a simple table of, say, 30 names, you could probably do so within a few seconds. A longer list might take minutes but it is still a practical task. However, if I asked you to compare a list of 100 names with a second list of 100 names, the task becomes a lot more laborious and prone to error.

Not only does the number of potential matches expand to 10,000 (100 × 100), but if you want to do so in one pass through the second table you have to hold all 100 names from the first table in your head—not easy!

Similarly, if I asked you to deduplicate a list of 100 names in a single list, you'd actually have to compare:

1. The first name against the remaining 99, then
2. The second name against the remaining 98 and so on.

In fact, you'd have 4,950 comparisons to make. At one per second that's about 80 minutes of work just to compare two short lists. For much larger datasets, the number of potential combinations becomes impractical, even for the most performant hardware.

Blind Matching?

So far we have assumed that the sets of data we seek to match are fully transparent to us—that the values of the attributes are readily available, in full, and have not been obscured or masked in any way. In some cases this ideal is not possible due to privacy constraints or geopolitical factors that prevent data from moving across borders. How can we find matches without being able to see the data? This feels like magic, but as we will see in Chapter 10, there are cryptographic techniques that enable matching to still take place without requiring full exposure of the list to be matched against.

The Entity Resolution Process

To overcome the challenges mentioned, the basic entity resolution process is divided into four sequential steps:

1. Data standardization
2. Record blocking
3. Attribute comparison
4. Match classification

After match classification additional postprocessing steps may be required:

- Clustering
- Canonicalization

Let's describe each of these steps briefly in turn.

Data Standardization

Before we can compare records we need to ensure that we have consistent data structures so that we can test for equivalence between attributes. We also need to ensure that the formatting of those attributes is consistent. This processing step usually involves splitting fields and removing null values and extraneous characters. It is often bespoke to the source dataset.

Record Blocking

To overcome the challenge of impractically high volumes of record comparisons, a process called *blocking* is often used. Instead of comparing every record with every other record, only subsets of record pairs, preselected based on ready equivalence between certain attributes, are compared in their entirety. This filtering approach concentrates the resolution process on those records with the highest propensity to match.

Attribute Comparison

The process of comparing individual attributes between the pairs of records selected by the blocking process occurs next. The degree of equivalence can be established based on an exact match between attributes or a similarity function. This process produces a set of equivalence measures between two record pairs.

Match Classification

The final step in the basic entity resolution process is to conclude whether the collective similarity between individual attributes is sufficient to declare two records a match, i.e., to resolve that they refer to the same real-world entity. This judgment can be made according to a set of manually defined rules or can be based on a machine learning probabilistic approach.

Clustering

Once our match classification is complete, we may group our records into connected clusters via their matching pairs. The inclusion of a record pair in a cluster may be determined by an additional match confidence threshold. Records without pairs above this threshold will form standalone clusters. If our matching criteria allow for different equivalence criteria, then our clusters may be intransitive; i.e., record A may be paired with record B, and record B paired with record C, but record C may not be paired to record A. As a result, clusters may be highly interconnected or more loosely coupled.

Canonicalization

Post resolution there may be a need to determine which attribute values should be used to represent an entity. If approximate matching techniques have been used to determine equivalence, or if an additional variable attribute is present in the pair or cluster but has not been used in the matching process, then there may be a need to decide which value is the most representative. The resulting canonical attribute values are then used to describe the resolved entity in onward calculations.

Worked Example

Returning to our simple example, let's apply the steps to our data. First, let's standardize our data, splitting the name attribute, standardizing the date of birth, and removing the extra characters in the place of birth and mobile number fields. Table 1-6 shows our cleansed records.

Table 1-6. Step 1: Data standardized records

First name	Last name	Date of birth	Place of birth	Mobile number
Michael	Shearer	1/4/1970	Stow on the Wold	07700 900999
Micheal	Shearer	1/14/1970	Stow on the Wold	07700 900999

In this simple example, we have only one pair to consider, so we don't need to apply blocking. We'll return to this in Chapter 5.

Next we'll compare the individual attributes for exact matches. Table 1-7 shows the comparison between each attribute as either a "Match" or a "No match."

Table 1-7. Step 3: Attribute comparison

Attribute	Value record 1	Value record 2	Comparison
First name	Michael	Micheal	No match
Last name	Shearer	Shearer	Match
Date of birth	1/4/1970	1/14/1970	No match
Place of birth	Stow on the Wold	Stow on the Wold	Match
Mobile number	07700 900999	07700 900999	Match

Finally, we apply step 4 to determine whether we have an overall match. A simple rule might be if the majority of the attributes match, then we conclude the overall record is a match, as in this case.

Alternatively, we might consider various combinations of matching attributes to be sufficient for us to declare a match. In our example, to declare a match we could look for either:

- Name match AND (date of birth OR place of birth match), or
- Name match AND mobile number match

We can take this approach a step further and assign a *relative weighting* to each of our attribute comparisons; a mobile number match is worth perhaps twice as much as a date of birth match, and so on. Combining these weighted scores produces an overall match score that can be considered against a given confidence threshold.

We will look more at different approaches to determine these relative weightings, using statistical techniques and machine learning, in Chapter 4.

As we have seen, different attributes may be stronger or weaker in helping us determine whether we have a match. Earlier, we considered the likelihood of finding a match for a name that is quite common versus one that is found more infrequently. For example, in a UK context, a match on a last name of Smith is likely to be less informative than a match on Shearer—there are fewer Shearers than Smiths, so a match is inherently less likely to begin with (a lower prior probability).

This probabilistic approach works particularly well when some of the values of a categorical attribute (one with a finite set of values) are significantly more common than others. If we consider a city attribute as part of an address match in a UK dataset, then London is likely to occur much more frequently than, say, Bath, and therefore may be weighted less.

Note that we haven't been able to determine which date of birth is definitively correct, so we are left with a canonicalization challenge.

Measuring Performance

Statistical approaches may help us to decide how to evaluate and combine all the clues that comparing individual attributes gives us, but how do we decide whether the combination is good enough or not? How do we set the confidence threshold to declare a match? This depends on what is important to us and how we propose to use our newly found matches.

Do we care more about being sure we spot every potential match and we are OK if in the process we declare a few matches that turn out to be false? This measure is known as *recall*. Or we don't want to waste our time with incorrect matches but if we miss a few true matches along the way that's OK. This is called *precision*.

When comparing two records, there are four different scenarios that can arise. Table 1-8 lists the different combinations of match decision and ground truth.

Table 1-8. Matching classifications

You decide	Ground truth	Instance of
Match	Match	True positive (TP)
Match	Not match	False positive (FP)
Not match	Match	False negative (FN)
Not match	Not match	True negative (TN)

If our recall measure is high, then we are only declaring relatively few false negatives, i.e., when we declare a match we rarely overlook a good candidate. If our precision is high, then when we declare a match we nearly always get it right.

At one extreme, imagine we declare every candidate pair a match; we would have zero false negatives and our measure of recall would be a perfect (1.0); we'd never overlook a match. Of course our precision would be very poor as we'd declare lots of nonmatches incorrectly as matches. Alternatively, imagine we declare a match in the ideal case, when every attribute is exactly equivalent; then we will never declare a match in error and our precision will be perfect (1.0), at the expense of our recall, which will be very poor as a lot of good matches pass us by.

Ideally, of course, we'd like high recall and precision simultaneously—our matches are both correct and comprehensive—but this is tricky to achieve! Chapter 6 describes this process in more detail.

Getting Started

So, how can we solve these challenges?

Hopefully this chapter has given you a good understanding of what entity resolution is, why it is needed, and the main steps in the process. Subsequent chapters will guide you, hands-on, through a set of worked real-world examples based on publicly available data.

Fortunately, in addition to commercial options, there are several open source Python libraries that do much of the hard work for us. These frameworks provide the scaffolding upon which we can construct a bespoke matching process that suits our data and context.

Before we begin, we'll take a short detour in the next chapter to set up our analytic environment and review some of the foundational Python data science libraries we will use, and then we'll consider the first step in our entity resolution process—standardizing our data ready for matching.

CHAPTER 2

Data Standardization

As we discussed in Chapter 1, before we can successfully match or deduplicate data sources we need to ensure our data is presented in a consistent manner and that any anomalies are removed or corrected. We will use the term *data standardization* to cover both the transformation of datasets into consistent formats and the cleansing of data to remove unhelpful extra characters that would otherwise interfere with the matching process.

In this chapter, we will get hands on and work through a real-world example of this process. We will create our working environment, acquire the data we need, cleanse that data, and then perform a simple entity resolution exercise to allow us to perform some simple analysis. We will conclude by examining the performance of our data matching process and consider how we might improve it.

First, let's introduce our example and why we need entity resolution to solve it.

Sample Problem

Let's work through an example problem to illustrate some of the common challenges we see in resolving entities between data sources and why data cleansing is an essential first step. As we are constrained to use openly available public sources of data, the example is slightly contrived but hopefully illustrates the need for entity resolution.

Let's imagine we are researching factors that may influence whether members of the House of Commons, the lower house of the Parliament of the United Kingdom (UK), are reelected. We surmise that politicians with an active social media presence might be more successful in securing reelection. For the purposes of this example, we are going to consider Facebook presence, and so we look at the last UK general election and examine how many politicians who held onto their seat have Facebook accounts.

Wikipedia has a web page that lists the members of Parliament (MPs) returned at the 2019 general election, including whether they were reelected, but it lacks social media information for those individuals. However, the TheyWorkForYou website (*https://theyworkforyou.com*) does record information on current MPs, including links to their Facebook accounts. So if we combine these datasets we can begin to test our hypothesis that reelection and social media presence are related.

TheyWorkForYou

TheyWorkForYou was founded to make Parliament more accessible and accountable. TheyWorkForYou is run by mySociety, a UK charity that puts power in more people's hands through the use of digital tools and data.

How can we join these two datasets? Although both datasets include the name of the constituency that each MP represents, we can't use this as a common key, because since the 2019 general election, a number of by-elections have taken place, returning new MPs.[1] These new members may have Facebook accounts but should not be considered in the reelection population as this might skew our analysis. Therefore, we need to connect our data by matching the names of the MPs between the two sets of records, i.e., resolving these entities so that we can create a single combined record for each MP.

Environment Setup

Our first task is to set up our entity resolution environment. In this book, we will be using Python and the JupyterLab IDE.

To begin, you'll need Python installed on your machine. If you don't already have it, you can download it from their website (*http://www.python.org*).[2]

Add Python to PATH

If installing Python for the first time, make sure to select the "Add Python to PATH" option to ensure you can run Python from your command line.

---

1 A by-election, also known as a special election in the United States, is an election used to fill an office that has become vacant between general elections. In the UK Parliament, a seat in the House of Commons can become vacant when an MP resigns or dies.

2 Software products identified in this book are suggestions only. You are responsible for evaluating whether to use any particular software and accept its license terms.

To download the code examples that accompany this book it is convenient to use the Git version control system. A guide to installing Git can be found on the GitHub website (*https://github.com/git-guides/install-git*).

Once Git is installed, you can clone (that is, take a copy of) the GitHub repository that accompanies this book onto your machine. Run this command from the parent directory of your choice:

```
>>>git clone https://github.com/mshearer0/HandsOnEntityResolution
```

This will create a subdirectory called *HandsOnEntityResolution*.

Python Virtual Environment

I recommend you use a virtual Python environment to work through the examples in this book. This will allow you to maintain the necessary Python package configuration without interfering with any other projects you may have. The following command creates a new environment in the *HandsOnEntityResolution* directory created by Git:

```
>>>python -m venv HandsOnEntityResolution
```

To activate the environment, run the following:

```
>>>.\HandsOnEntityResolution\Scripts\activate.bat
(Windows)
```

```
>>>source HandsOnEntityResolution/bin/activate
(Linux)
```

This will prefix your command prompt to show the environment name based on the directory name:

```
>>>(HandsOnEntityResolution)
   your_path\HandsOnEntityResolution
```

Once you've finished, it's important to deactivate the environment:

```
>>>deactivate (Windows)
```

```
>>>deactivate (Linux)
```

Next, change into this directory:

```
>>>cd HandsOnEntityResolution
```

To set up our JupyterLab code environment and the packages required, we will use the Python package manager pip, which should be included with your Python installation. You can check using:

```
>>>python -m pip --version
pip 23.0.1 from your_path\HandsOnEntityResolution\lib\
   site-packages\pip (python 3.7)
```

You can then install the packages you will need throughout the book from the *requirements.txt* file using:

```
>>>pip install -r requirements.txt
```

Next, configure a Python kernel associated with our virtual environment for our notebooks to pick up:

```
>>>python -m ipykernel install --user
   --name=handsonentityresolution
```

Then start JupyterLab with:

```
>>>jupyter-lab
```

While it's pretty self-explanatory, instructions on how to get started with Jupyter are available in the documentation (*https://docs.jupyter.org/en/latest*).

Acquiring Data

Now that we have our environment configured, our next task is to acquire the data we need. It's often the case that the data we need comes in a variety of formats and presentations. The examples included in this book will illustrate how to deal with some of the most common formats we encounter.

Wikipedia Data

Opening *Chapter2.ipynb* in our Jupyter environment, we start by defining the Wikipedia URL for the list of MPs returned in the 2019 UK general election:

```
url = "https://en.wikipedia.org/wiki/
       List_of_MPs_elected_in_the_2019_United_Kingdom_general_election"
```

Then we can import the requests and Beautiful Soup Python packages and use them to download a copy of the Wikipedia text. Then run an `html parser` to extract all the tables present on the page:

```
import requests
from bs4 import BeautifulSoup

website_url = requests.get(url).text
soup = BeautifulSoup(website_url,'html.parser')
tables = soup.find_all('table')
```

Beautiful Soup

Beautiful Soup is a Python package that makes it easy to scrape information from web pages. More details are available online (*https://oreil.ly/YB8H3*).

Next, we need to find the table we want within the page. In this case we select the table that includes the text "Member returned" (a column name). Within this table, we extract the column names as headers and then iterate through all the remaining rows and elements, building a list of lists. These lists are then loaded into a pandas DataFrame, setting the extracted headers as DataFrame column names:

```python
import pandas as pd

for table in tables:
    if 'Member returned' in table.text:
        headers = [header.text.strip() for header in table.find_all('th')]
        headers = headers[:5]
        dfrows = []
        table_rows = table.find_all('tr')
        for row in table_rows:
            td = row.find_all('td')
            dfrow = [row.text for row in td if row.text!='\n']
            dfrows.append(dfrow)

df_w = pd.DataFrame(dfrows, columns=headers)
```

The result is a pandas DataFrame, shown in Figure 2-1, which we can examine using the info method.

```
In [3]: df_w.info()

        <class 'pandas.core.frame.DataFrame'>
        RangeIndex: 652 entries, 0 to 651
        Data columns (total 5 columns):
         #   Column                         Non-Null Count   Dtype
        ---  ------                         --------------   -----
         0   Constituency                   650 non-null     object
         1   Party of incumbentbefore election  650 non-null     object
         2   Member returned                650 non-null     object
         3   Party of incumbentafter election   650 non-null     object
         4   Notes                          650 non-null     object
        dtypes: object(5)
        memory usage: 25.6+ KB
```

Figure 2-1. Wikipedia MP information

We have 652 entries of 5 columns. This looks encouraging because in each column, 650 rows have nonnull values, which matches the number of UK House of Commons parliamentary constituencies.

Finally, we can simplify our dataset by retaining only the columns we need:

```python
df_w = df_w[['Constituency','Member returned','Notes']]
```

TheyWorkForYou Data

Now we can move on to downloading our second dataset and loading it into a separate DataFrame, as shown in Figure 2-2:

```
url = "https://www.theyworkforyou.com/mps/?f=csv"
df_t = pd.read_csv(url, header=0)
```

```
In [7]: df_t.info()

        <class 'pandas.core.frame.DataFrame'>
        RangeIndex: 650 entries, 0 to 649
        Data columns (total 7 columns):
         #   Column         Non-Null Count   Dtype
        ---  ------         --------------   -----
         0   Unnamed: 0     650 non-null     int64
         1   Person ID      650 non-null     int64
         2   First name     650 non-null     object
         3   Last name      650 non-null     object
         4   Party          650 non-null     object
         5   Constituency   650 non-null     object
         6   URI            650 non-null     object
        dtypes: int64(2), object(5)
        memory usage: 35.7+ KB
```

Figure 2-2. TheyWorkForYou MP information

Post 2024/25 UK General Election

If you're reading this book after the 2024/25 UK general election, then the TheyWorkForYou website will likely be updated with the new MPs. If you're following along on your own machine, then please use the *mps_they_raw.csv* file supplied in the GitHub repository that accompanies this book. The raw Wikipedia data *mps_wiki_raw.csv* is also provided.

Figure 2-3 lists the first few rows of the DataFrame so that we can see information these fields typically contain.

```
In [8]: df_t.head(n=5)
```

	Unnamed: 0	Person ID	First name	Last name	Party	Constituency	URI
0	0	10001	Diane	Abbott	Labour	Hackney North and Stoke Newington	https://www.theyworkforyou.com/mp/10001/diane_...
1	1	25034	Debbie	Abrahams	Labour	Oldham East and Saddleworth	https://www.theyworkforyou.com/mp/25034/debbie...
2	2	24878	Nigel	Adams	Conservative	Selby and Ainsty	https://www.theyworkforyou.com/mp/24878/nigel_...
3	3	25661	Bim	Afolami	Conservative	Hitchin and Harpenden	https://www.theyworkforyou.com/mp/25661/bim_af...
4	4	11929	Adam	Afriyie	Conservative	Windsor	https://www.theyworkforyou.com/mp/11929/adam_a...

Figure 2-3. First five rows of the TheyWorkForYou dataset

To discover whether each MP has an associated Facebook account we need to follow the link in the URI column to look up their TheyWorkForYou homepage. We'll need to do this for each row, so we define a function that we can apply along the axis of the DataFrame.

Adding Facebook links

The function uses the same Beautiful Soup package we used to parse the Wikipedia web page. In this case, we extract all the links to *facebook.com*. We then examine the first link. If this link is the account of TheyWorkForYou, then the site doesn't have a Facebook account listed for the MP, so we return a nil string; if it does, then we return that link:

```
def facelink(url):
    website_url = requests.get(url).text
    soup = BeautifulSoup(website_url,'html.parser')
    flinks = [f"{item['href']}" for item in soup.select
        ("a[href*='facebook.com']")]
    if flinks[0]!="https://www.facebook.com/TheyWorkForYou":
        return(flinks[0])
    else:
        return("")
```

We can apply this function to every row in the DataFrame using the `apply` method to call the `facelink` function, passing the URI value as the URL. The value returned from the function is added to a new column that Flink appended to the DataFrame.

```
df_t['Flink'] = df_t.apply(lambda x: facelink(x.URI), axis=1)
```

Be patient—this function has to do quite a bit of work, so it may take a few minutes to run on your machine. Once this completes we can view the first few rows again, as shown in Figure 2-4, to check if we are getting the Facebook links we expect.

```
In [11]: df_t.head(n=5)
Out[11]:
```

	Unnamed: 0	Person ID	First name	Last name	Party	Constituency	URI	Flink
0	0	10001	Diane	Abbott	Labour	Hackney North and Stoke Newington	https://www.theyworkforyou.com/mp/10001/diane_...	https://facebook.com/Dianeabbott
1	1	25034	Debbie	Abrahams	Labour	Oldham East and Saddleworth	https://www.theyworkforyou.com/mp/25034/debbie...	
2	2	24878	Nigel	Adams	Conservative	Selby and Ainsty	https://www.theyworkforyou.com/mp/24878/nigel_...	https://facebook.com/nigel.adamsmp
3	3	25861	Bim	Afolami	Conservative	Hitchin and Harpenden	https://www.theyworkforyou.com/mp/25861/bim_af...	
4	4	11929	Adam	Afriyie	Conservative	Windsor	https://www.theyworkforyou.com/mp/11929/adam_a...	https://facebook.com/adamafriyieofficial

Figure 2-4. First five rows of the TheyWorkForYou dataset with Facebook links

Finally, we can simplify our dataset by retaining only the columns we need:

```
df_t = df_t[['Constituency','First name','Last name','Flink']]
```

Cleansing Data

Now that we have our raw datasets we can begin our data cleansing process. We will perform some initial cleansing on the Wikipedia dataset first and then the TheyWorkForYou data. We will then attempt to join these datasets and see what further inconsistencies are revealed that we need to standardize.

Wikipedia

Let's have a look at the first and last few rows in the Wikipedia dataset, as shown in Figure 2-5.

```
In [13]: df_w.head(n=5)
Out[13]:
```

	Constituency	Member returned	Notes
0	None	None	None
1	Aberavon\n	Stephen Kinnock\n	Seat held\n
2	Aberconwy\n	Robin Millar\n	Previous incumbent, Guto Bebb, did not stand\n
3	Aberdeen North\n	Kirsty Blackman\n	Seat held\n
4	Aberdeen South\n	Stephen Flynn\n	Previous incumbent, Ross Thomson, did not stand\n

```
In [14]: df_w.tail(n=5)
Out[14]:
```

	Constituency	Member returned	Notes
647	Yeovil\n	Marcus Fysh\n	Seat held\n
648	Ynys Môn\n	Virginia Crosbie\n	Previous incumbent, Albert Owen, did not stand\n
649	York Central\n	Rachael Maskell\n	Seat held\n
650	York Outer\n	Julian Sturdy\n	Seat held\n
651	None	None	None

Figure 2-5. First and last 5 rows of the Wikipedia data

The first task in our cleansing process is to standardize our column names:

```
df_w = df_w.rename(columns={ 'Member returned' : 'Fullname'})
```

We can also see that the output of our parser has a blank row at the start and end of our DataFrame, and it appears we have \n characters appended to each element. These additions would clearly interfere with our match, so they need to be removed.

To remove the blank rows we can use:

```
df = df.dropna()
```

To remove the trailing \n characters:

```
df_w['Constituency'] = df_w['Constituency'].str.rstrip("\n")
df_w['Fullname'] = df_w['Fullname'].str.rstrip("\n")
```

To be sure we now have a clean Fullname we can check for any other \n characters.

```
df_w[df_w['Fullname'].astype(str).str.contains('\n')]
```

This simple check shows that we also have leading values that we need to remove:

```
df_w['Fullname'] = df_w['Fullname'].str.lstrip("\n")
```

Our next task is to split our Fullname into Firstname and Lastname so that we can match these values independently. For the purposes of this example, we are going to use a simple method, selecting the first substring as the Firstname and the remaining substrings, separated by spaces, as the Lastname.

```
df_w['Firstname'] = df_w['Fullname'].str.split().str[0]
df_w['Lastname'] = df_w['Fullname'].astype(str).apply(lambda x:
    ' '.join(x.split()[1:]))
```

We can check how well this basic method has worked by looking for Lastname entries that contain spaces. Figure 2-6 shows the remaining Lastname entries with spaces present.

```
In [21]:  # Check for compound lastnames

          df_w[df_w['Lastname'].astype(str).str.contains(' ')]['Lastname']

Out[21]:  31        de Cordova
          134     Duncan Smith
          393     Marie Morris
          592       Ahmad Khan
          Name: Lastname, dtype: object
```

Figure 2-6. Check for compound Lastname entries in Wikipedia data

We now have a sufficiently clean dataset to attempt a first match, so we'll move on to our second dataset.

TheyWorkForYou

As we saw earlier, the TheyWorkForYou data is already pretty clean, so at this stage all we need to do is standardize the column names with those of the previous DataFrame. This will make our life easier as we attempt to match:

```
df_t = df_t.rename(columns={'Last name' : 'Lastname',
                            'First name' : 'Firstname'})
```

Attribute Comparison

Now that we have two similarly formatted DataFrames, we can experiment with the next stage of the entity resolution process. Because our datasets are small we don't need to employ record blocking, and so we can proceed directly to try a simple exact match of `Firstname`, `Lastname`, and `Constituency`. The `merge` method (similar to a database `join`) does this exact matching for us:

```
len(df_w.merge(df_t, on=['Constituency','Firstname','Lastname']))
599
```

We find that 599 of 650 are perfect matches of all three attributes—not bad! Matching on just `Constituency` and `Lastname` gives us 607 perfect matches, so we clearly have 8 mismatching `Firstname` entries:

```
len(df_w.merge(df_t, on=['Constituency','Lastname']))
607
```

Repeating the process for the remaining permutations of `Firstname`, `Lastname`, and `Constituency` gives us the Venn diagram of match counts shown in Figure 2-7.

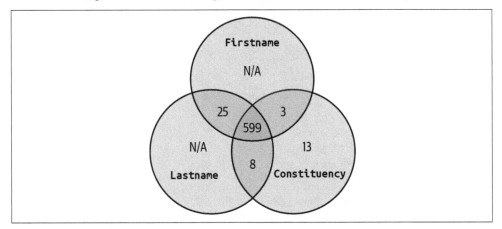

Figure 2-7. Venn diagram

A simple join on `Firstname` gives 2,663 matches and the equivalent match on `Lastname` has 982 matches. These counts exceed the number of MPs and arise because of repeated common names that match more than once between the two datasets.

We have 599 matches out of 650 so far, but can we do better? Let's start with examining the `Constituency` attribute in our datasets. As a categorical variable, we would expect this to be pretty easy to match:

```
len(df_w.merge(df_t, on=['Constituency'] ))
623
```

We have 623 matches, leaving 27 unmatched. Why? Surely we'd expect the same constituencies to be present in both datasets, so what is going wrong?

Constituency

Let's have a look at the first five of the unmatched population in both datasets. To do this we perform an outer join between the DataFrames using the `Constituency` attribute and then select those records found in either the right (Wikipedia) or left (TheyWorkForYou) DataFrame. The results are shown in Figure 2-8.

```
In [33]: df_w_outer = df_w.merge(df_t, on=['Constituency'],how="outer",indicator=True)
         df_w_outer[df_w_outer['_merge']=='right_only']['Constituency'].head(n=5)

Out[33]: 650    Birmingham, Hall Green
         651        Liverpool, Wavertree
         652           Sheffield, Hallam
         653        Liverpool, West Derby
         654    Birmingham, Hodge Hill
         Name: Constituency, dtype: object


In [34]: df_w_outer[df_w_outer['_merge']=='left_only']['Constituency'].head(n=5)

Out[34]: 46    Birmingham Edgbaston
         47    Birmingham Erdington
         48    Birmingham Hall Green
         49    Birmingham Hodge Hill
         50       Birmingham Ladywood
         Name: Constituency, dtype: object
```

Figure 2-8. Constituency mismatches

We can see that the first dataset from the TheyWorkForYou website has commas embedded in the constituency names, whereas the Wikipedia data does not. This explains why they don't match. To ensure consistency, let's remove any commas from both DataFrames:

```
df_t['Constituency'] = df_t['Constituency'].str.replace(',', '')
df_w['Constituency'] = df_w['Constituency'].str.replace(',', '')
```

After applying this cleansing we have a perfect match on all 650 constituencies:

```
len(df_w.merge(df_t, on=['Constituency']))
650
```

 Case Sensitivity

In this simple example, we have matching case conventions (e.g., initial capitalization) between the two datasets. In many situations this won't be the case, and you'll need to standardize on upper- or lowercase characters. We'll see how this can be done in later chapters.

Repeating our perfect match on all three attributes, we can now match 624 records:

```
len(df_w.merge(df_t, on=['Constituency','Firstname','Lastname']))
624
```

What about the other 26?

A little domain knowledge is useful here. As we considered at the start of the chapter, between the election in 2019 and the time of writing, a number of by-elections took place. If we look at constituencies where neither the first name nor the last name matches then, for this simple example at least, we can identify likely candidates, as shown in Figure 2-9.

```
In [34]: df_w_inner = df_w.merge(df_t, on=['Constituency'], suffixes=('_w', '_t'))
         df_w_inner[(df_w_inner['Firstname_w'] != df_w_inner['Firstname_t']) & (df_w_inner['Lastname_w'] != df_w_inner['Lastname_t'])]
Out[34]:
```

	Constituency	Fullname	Notes	Firstname_w	Lastname_w	Firstname_t	Lastname_t	Flink
4	Airdrie and Shotts	Neil Gray	Seat held\n	Neil	Gray	Anum	Qaisar	
29	Batley and Spen	Tracy Brabin	Seat held\n	Tracy	Brabin	Kim	Leadbeater	
47	Birmingham Erdington	Jack Dromey	Seat held\n	Jack	Dromey	Paulette	Hamilton	
130	Chesham and Amersham	Cheryl Gillan	Seat held\n	Cheryl	Gillan	Sarah	Green	
139	City of Chester	Chris Matheson	Seat held\n	Chris	Matheson	Samantha	Dixon	
268	Hartlepool	Mike Hill	Seat held\n	Mike	Hill	Jill	Mortimer	
392	Newton Abbot	Anne Marie Morris	Seat held\n	Anne	Marie Morris	Anne Marie	Morris	https://facebook.com/annemarie.morris.NA
410	North Shropshire	Owen Paterson	Seat held\n	Owen	Paterson	Helen	Morgan	
432	Old Bexley and Sidcup	James Brokenshire	Seat held\n	James	Brokenshire	Louie	French	
531	Southend West	David Amess	Seat held\n	David	Amess	Anna	Firth	
555	Stretford and Urmston	Kate Green	Seat held\n	Kate	Green	Andrew	Western	
574	Tiverton and Honiton	Neil Parish	Seat held\n	Neil	Parish	Richard	Foord	
591	Wakefield	Imran Ahmad Khan	Defeated incumbent, Mary Creagh\n	Imran	Ahmad Khan	Simon	Lightwood	
617	West Lancashire	Rosie Cooper	Seat held\n	Rosie	Cooper	Ashley	Dalton	

Figure 2-9. Potential by-elections

Of our 14 by-election candidates, we have 13 cases where the names are entirely different, suggesting we are correct to discount them, but the candidate for Newton Abbot appears to be a potential match because the middle name "Morris" has been included in the last name in one dataset and in the first name in the other, frustrating our exact match on both attributes.

In fact, we can verify our conclusion with data from the UK Parliament website (*https://oreil.ly/eWhWf*). This confirms that by-elections have been held in the matching constituencies. So this explains 13 of our 26 unmatched records—what about the rest? Let's pick out where either the first name or the last name matches but the other doesn't. This subset is shown in Figure 2-10.

```
In [35]: df_w_inner = df_w.merge(df_t, on=['Constituency'], suffixes=('_w', '_t'))
         df_w_inner[(df_w_inner['Firstname_w'] == df_w_inner['Firstname_t']) & (df_w_inner['Lastname_w'] != df_w_inner['Lastname_t']) |
             (df_w_inner['Firstname_w'] != df_w_inner['Firstname_t']) & (df_w_inner['Lastname_w'] == df_w_inner['Lastname_t'])]
```

Out[35]:

	Constituency	Fullname	Notes	Firstname_w	Lastname_w	Firstname_t	Lastname_t	Flink
48	Birmingham Edgbaston	Preet Gill	Seat held'n	Preet	Gill	Preet Kaur	Gill	https://facebook.com/PreetKaurGillMP
99	Burton	Kate Griffiths	Previous incumbent, Andrew Griffiths, did not ...	Kate	Griffiths	Kate	Kniveton	
122	Central Suffolk and North Ipswich	Dan Poulter	Seat held'n	Dan	Poulter	Daniel	Poulter	
777	Hayes and Harlington	McDonnell	Seat held'n	John	McDonnell	John Martin	McDonnell	https://facebook.com/johnmcdonnellmp
311	Kingston upon Hull North	Diana Johnson	Seat held'n	Diana	Johnson	Diana R.	Johnson	https://facebook.com/DianaJohnsonHullNorth
316	Lagan Valley	Jeffrey Donaldson	Seat held'n	Jeffrey	Donaldson	Jeffrey M.	Donaldson	https://facebook.com/jeffrey.donaldson1
394	North Antrim	Ian Paisley	Seat held'n	Ian	Paisley	Ian	Paisley Jnr	
502	Slough	Tanmanjeet Dhesi	Seat held'n	Tanmanjeet	Dhesi	Tan	Dhesi	https://facebook.com/tandhesi
510	South Down	Chris Hazzard	Seat held'n	Chris	Hazzard	Christopher	Hazzard	https://facebook.com/chris.hazzard.77
526	South West Norfolk	Liz Truss	Seat held'n	Liz	Truss	Elizabeth	Truss	https://facebook.com/ElizabethTrussSWNorfolk
605	Wealden	Nus Ghani	Seat held'n	Nus	Ghani	Nusrat	Ghani	https://facebook.com/NusGhaniofficial
615	West Dunbartonshire	Martin Docherty-Hughes	Seat held'n	Martin	Docherty-Hughes	Martin	Docherty	https://facebook.com/MartinDochertySNP

Figure 2-10. Potential by-elections

We can see that the remaining 12 records, as listed in Table 2-1, display a variety of the matching issues that we discussed in Chapter 1.

Table 2-1. Matching issues summary table

Matching issue	TheyWorkForYou	Wikipedia
Shortened names	Dan	Daniel
	Tan	Tanmanjeet
	Liz	Elizabeth
	Chris	Christopher
	Nus	Nusrat
Middle initials included	Diana R.	Diana
	Jeffrey M.	Jeffrey
Middle name included	Preet Kaur	Preet
	John Martin	John
Last name suffix	Paisley Jnr	Paisley
Double-barreled last names	Docherty	Docherty-Hughes

There is one remaining mismatch that is really hard to resolve: a change of the last name Kniveton (previously Griffiths) in the Burton constituency. Now we have accounted for all 650 constituencies.

If we further cleanse the `Firstname` from the TheyWorkForYou data, removing any middle initials or names, we can improve our matches still further:

```
df_t['Firstname'] = df_t['Firstname'].str.split().str[0]
```

We can now match another four records:

```
df_resolved = df_w.merge(df_t, on=['Firstname','Lastname'] )

len(df_resolved)
628
```

This brings us to end of our introduction to basic data cleansing techniques. We now have only nine unresolved records, as shown in Figure 2-11. In the next chapter, we will see how more approximate text matching techniques can help us resolve some of these too.

```
In [38]: df_w_inner = df_w.merge(df_t, on=['Constituency'], suffixes=('_w', '_t'))
         df_w_unmatched = df_w_inner[(df_w_inner['Firstname_w'] == df_w_inner['Firstname_t']) & (df_w_inner['Lastname_w'] != df_w_inner['L
              (df_w_inner['Firstname_w'] != df_w_inner['Firstname_t']) & (df_w_inner['Lastname_w'] == df_w_inner['Lastname_t'])]
         df_w_unmatched
```

Out[38]:

	Constituency	Fullname	Notes	Firstname_w	Lastname_w	Firstname_t	Lastname_t	Flink
99	Burton	Kate Griffiths	Previous incumbent, Andrew Griffiths, did not ...	Kate	Griffiths	Kate	Kniveton	
122	Central Suffolk and North Ipswich	Dan Poulter	Seat held\n	Dan	Poulter	Daniel	Poulter	
392	Newton Abbot	Anne Marie Morris	Seat held\n	Anne	Marie Morris	Anne	Morris	https://facebook.com/annemarie.morris.NA
394	North Antrim	Ian Paisley	Seat held\n	Ian	Paisley	Ian	Paisley Jnr	
502	Slough	Tanmanjeet Dhesi	Seat held\n	Tanmanjeet	Dhesi	Tan	Dhesi	https://facebook.com/tandhesi
510	South Down	Chris Hazzard	Seat held\n	Chris	Hazzard	Christopher	Hazzard	https://facebook.com/chris.hazzard.77
526	South West Norfolk	Liz Truss	Seat held\n	Liz	Truss	Elizabeth	Truss	https://facebook.com/ElizabethTrussSWNorfolk
605	Wealden	Nus Ghani	Seat held\n	Nus	Ghani	Nusrat	Ghani	https://facebook.com/NusGhaniofficial
615	West Dunbartonshire	Martin Docherty-Hughes	Seat held\n	Martin	Docherty-Hughes	Martin	Docherty	https://facebook.com/MartinDochertySNP

Figure 2-11. Unresolved entities

Measuring Performance

Let's evaluate our performance using a simple exact matching method based on the metrics we defined in Chapter 1. Our total population size is 650, within which we have:

$$True\ positive\ matches\,(TP) = 628$$

$$False\ positive\ matches\,(FP) = 0$$

$$True\ negative\ matches\,(TN) = 13\,(By-elections)$$

$$False\ negative\ matches\,(FN) = 9$$

We can calculate our performance metrics as:

$$Precision = \frac{TP}{(TP+FP)} = \frac{628}{(628+0)} = 100\,\%$$

$$Recall = \frac{TP}{(TP + FN)} = \frac{628}{(628 + 9)} \approx 98.6\%$$

$$Accuracy = \frac{(TP + TN)}{(TP + TN + FP + FN)} = \frac{(628 + 13)}{650} \approx 98.6\%$$

Our precision is perfect because we are setting a very high bar—an exact match on first name, last name, and constituency; if we declare a match, we always get it right. Our recall is also extremely good; we rarely fail to find a match we should have found. Finally, our overall accuracy is also very high.

Of course, this is a simple example with relatively high-quality data and we have the advantage of a very strong categorical variable (constituency) to match against.

Sample Calculation

We have successfully resolved the names between our two datasets, so now we can use the combined information to test our hypothesis about the correlation between social media presence and the likelihood of reelection. Our resolved data now has everything we need in one table. Figure 2-12 shows the first few rows of this table.

	Constituency_x	Fullname	Notes	Firstname	Lastname	Constituency_y	Flink
0	Aberavon	Stephen Kinnock	Seat held\n	Stephen	Kinnock	Aberavon	https://facebook.com/stephenkinnock
1	Aberconwy	Robin Millar	Previous incumbent, Guto Bebb, did not stand\n	Robin	Millar	Aberconwy	
2	Aberdeen North	Kirsty Blackman	Seat held\n	Kirsty	Blackman	Aberdeen North	https://facebook.com/aberdeennorth
3	Aberdeen South	Stephen Flynn	Previous incumbent, Ross Thomson, did not stand\n	Stephen	Flynn	Aberdeen South	
4	Aldershot	Leo Docherty	Seat held\n	Leo	Docherty	Aldershot	https://facebook.com/pg/LeoDocherty4Aldershot

Figure 2-12. Sample of resolved entities

We can calculate the number of MPs who currently have Facebook accounts who held their seats in the 2019 election:

```
df_heldwithface = df_resolved[(df_resolved['Flink']!="") &
    (df_resolved['Notes']=="Seat held\n")]
len(df_heldwithface)
474
```

As a percentage: $\frac{474}{628} \approx 75\%$.

Finally, we'll save our cleansed datasets locally so that we can use them in subsequent chapters:

```
df_w.to_csv('mps_wiki_clean.csv', index=False)
df_t.to_csv('mps_they_clean.csv', index=False)
```

Summary

To summarize, we used five simple techniques to standardize and cleanse our data:

- Removed null records
- Removed leading and trailing unwanted characters
- Split full name into first name and last name
- Removed commas from constituency
- Removed middle names and initials from first name

As a result we were able to join our datasets and then calculate a simple metric that we otherwise could not. Alas, there is no ubiquitous cleansing process; it depends on the datasets you have.

In the next chapter we will see how fuzzy matching techniques can improve our performance even more.

CHAPTER 3

Text Matching

As we saw in Chapter 2, once our data is cleansed and consistently formatted, we can find matching entities by checking for exact matches between their data attributes. If the data is of high quality, and if the attribute values are nonrepetitive, then checking for equivalence is straightforward. However, this is rarely the case with real-world data.

We can increase our likelihood of matching all relevant records by using *approximate* (often referred to as *fuzzy*) *matching techniques*. For numerical values, we can set a tolerance on how close the values need to be. For example, a date of birth might be matched if it's within a few days or a location might be matched if its coordinates are within a certain distance apart. For textual data, we can look for similarities and differences between strings that could arise accidentally.

Of course, by accepting nonexact matches as equivalent we open up the possibility of matching records incorrectly.

In this chapter, we will introduce some frequently used text matching techniques and then apply them to our sample problem to see if this can improve our entity resolution performance.

Edit Distance Matching

For matching text, one of the most useful approximate matching techniques is to measure the *edit distance* between two strings. The edit distance is the minimum number of operations to transform one string into the other. This metric can therefore be used to assess the likelihood that two strings do actually describe the same attribute, even if they were recorded differently.

The first, and most universally applicable, approximate matching technique we will consider is the Levenshtein distance.

Levenshtein Distance

The *Levenshtein distance* is a well-known edit distance metric named after its creator, Soviet mathematician Vladimir Levenshtein.

The Levenshtein distance between two strings, a and b (of length |a| and |b|, respectively), is given by lev(a,b), where

$$
lev(a, b) = \begin{cases} |a| & \text{if } |b| = 0, \\ |b| & \text{if } |a| = 0, \\ lev(tail(a), tail(b)) & \text{if } a[0] = b[0], \\ 1 + min \begin{cases} lev(tail(a), b) \\ lev(a, tail(b)) \\ lev(tail(a), tail(b)) \end{cases} & \text{otherwise} \end{cases}
$$

Here, the tail of some string x is a string of all but the first character of x, and x[n] is the nth character of the string x, counting from 0.

Opening the *Chapter3.ipynb* notebook, we can see how this works in practice. Fortunately, we don't have to code the Levenshtein algorithm ourselves—the Jellyfish Python package has an implementation we can use. This library also contains a number of other fuzzy and phonetic string-matching functions.

Jellyfish

Jellyfish (*https://github.com/jamesturk/jellyfish*) is a Python library for approximate and phonetic matching of strings.

If you don't have this package installed, you can use a Jupyter Notebook magic command `%pip` to install it before importing:

```
%pip install jellyfish
import jellyfish as jf
```

Kernel Restart

After installing a new Python package, you may need to restart the kernel and rerun the notebook.

We can then calculate the edit distance metric to examine how a common misspelling error might be measured:

```
jf.levenshtein_distance('Michael','Micheal')
2
```

Logically, the Levenshtein algorithm iterates character by character through the characters of the two strings, from first to last, incrementing the distance score if the characters do not match. In this case as the M, i, c, and h characters all match, the first time we increment the distance score is when we encounter the mismatch of letters a and e on the fifth character. At this point we then iterate through three variants of the remaining characters, selecting the minimum score between residual strings:

"el" and "ael"
"ael" and "al"
"el" and "al"

All three options also have a mismatch on the next character, incrementing the score again. Repeating the process on each option generates three more suboptions, the last of which is a simple match between the final "l" of each string, for a total minimum score of 2.

I leave it as an exercise for the reader to work through the remaining options, all of which produce the same score of 2.

Jaro Similarity

An alternative method of assessing the similarity of strings was suggested by Matthew Jaro in 1989. Wikipedia gives the formula as follows.

The Jaro similarity sim_j of two strings s_1 and s_2 is

$$sim_j = \begin{cases} 0 & \text{if } m = 0 \\ \frac{1}{3}\left(\frac{m}{|s_1|} + \frac{m}{|s_2|} + \frac{m-t}{m}\right) & \text{otherwise} \end{cases}$$

where:

- $|s_i|$ is the length of the string s_i
- m is the number of matching characters (see below)
- t is the number of transpositions (see below)
- Jaro similarity score is 0 if the strings do not match at all, and 1 if they are an exact match.

In the first step, each character of s_1 is compared with all its matching characters in s_2. Two characters from s_1 and s_2, respectively, are considered matching only if they are the same and not farther than $\left\lfloor \frac{max(s_1, s_2)}{2} \right\rfloor - 1$ characters apart. If no matching characters are found, then the strings are not similar and the algorithm terminates by returning Jaro similarity score 0. If nonzero matching characters are found, the next step is to find the number of transpositions. Transposition is the number of matching characters that are not in the right order divided by two.

Again we can use the Jellyfish library to calculate this for us:

```
jf.jaro_similarity('Michael','Micheal')
0.9523809523809524
```

Here the value is calculated as:

$|s_1| = |s_2| = 7$ (length of both strings)
$m = 7$ (all characters match)
$t = 1$ (a and e transposition)

Therefore, the Jaro similarity value is calculated as:

$$= \frac{1}{3}\left(\frac{7}{7} + \frac{7}{7} + \frac{(7-1)}{7}\right) = \frac{20}{21} = 0.9523809523809524 \,.$$

In both the Levenshtein and Jaro methods all the characters in a string contribute equally to the score. Often, however, when matching names, the first few characters are more significant. Therefore, if they are the same, they are more likely to indicate equivalence. To recognize this, a modification of the Jaro similarity was proposed by William E. Winkler in 1990.

Jaro-Winkler Similarity

Jaro-Winkler similarity uses a prefix scale p that gives more favorable ratings to strings that match from the beginning for a set prefix length l. Given two strings s_1 and s_2 their Jaro-Winkler similarity sim_w is $sim_w = sim_j + lp(1 - sim_j)$, where:

- sim_j is the Jaro similarity for s_1 and s_2.
- l is the length of common prefix at the start of the string up to a maximum of four characters.
- p is a constant scaling factor for how much the score is adjusted upward for having common prefixes.

- *p* should not exceed 0.25 (i.e., 1/4, with 4 being the maximum length of the prefix being considered); otherwise the similarity could become larger than 1.
- The standard value for this constant in Winkler's work is $p = 0.1$.

Using this metric:

```
jf.jaro_winkler_similarity('Michael','Micheal')
```

```
0.9714285714285714
```

which is calculated as follows:

$$= \frac{20}{21} + 4 \times 0.1 \times \left(1 - \frac{20}{21}\right) = 0.9714285714285714$$

where:

- $sim_j = \frac{20}{21}$
- $l = 4$ (common prefix of "Mich")
- $p = 0.1$ (standard value)

It is worth noting that Jaro-Winkler similarity measures are case sensitive, so:

```
jf.jaro_winkler_similarity('michael','MICHAEL')
0
```

A common practice is therefore to convert strings to lowercase before matching.

```
jf.jaro_winkler_similarity('michael'.lower(),'MICHAEL'.lower())
1.0
```

Phonetic Matching

An alternative to edit distance matching is to compare how similarly words are pronounced. Most of these phonetic algorithms are based on English pronunciation, of which two of the most popular are *Metaphone* and *Match Rating Approach (MRA)*.

Metaphone

The Metaphone algorithm encodes each word into a sequence of letters from the set of "0BFHJKLMNPRSTWXY" where 0 represents the "th" sound and X represents "sh" or "ch." For example, using the Jellyfish package, we can see 'michael' is reduced to 'MXL' as is 'michel'.

```
jf.metaphone('michael')
MXL
```

This transformation produces a common key that can then be exact-matched to determine equivalence.

Match Rating Approach

The MRA phonetic algorithm was developed in the late 1970s. Like Metaphone, it uses a set of rules to encode a word into a simplified phonetic representation. A set of comparison rules are then used to assess similarity, which is evaluated against a minimum threshold derived from their combined lengths to determine whether there is a match.

Comparing the Techniques

To compare the edit distance and phonetic similarity techniques, let's examine how well they evaluate common misspellings and abbreviations of Michael:

```
mylist = ['Michael','Micheal','Michel','Mike','Mick']
combs = []

import itertools

for a, b in itertools.combinations(mylist, 2):
    combs.append([a,b,
        jf.jaro_similarity(a,b),
        jf.jaro_winkler_similarity(a, b),
        jf.levenshtein_distance(a,b),
        jf.match_rating_comparison(a,b),
        (jf.metaphone(a)==jf.metaphone(b))])

pd.DataFrame(combs, columns=['Name1','Name2','Jaro','JaroWinkler','Levenshtein',
    'Match Rating','Metaphone'])
```

This gives us the results shown in Table 3-1.

Table 3-1. Text matching comparison

Name1	Name2	Jaro	Jaro-Winkler	Levenshtein	Match rating	Metaphone
Michael	Micheal	0.952381	0.971429	2	True	True
Michael	Michel	0.952381	0.971429	1	True	True
Michael	Mike	0.726190	0.780952	4	False	False
Michael	Mick	0.726190	0.808333	4	True	False
Micheal	Michel	0.952381	0.971429	1	True	True
Micheal	Mike	0.726190	0.780952	4	False	False
Micheal	Mick	0.726190	0.780952	4	True	False
Michel	Mike	0.750000	0.808333	3	False	False
Michel	Mick	0.750000	0.825000	3	True	False
Mike	Mick	0.833333	0.866667	2	True	True

As we can see just from this trivial example, there is a fair degree of consistency between the techniques but there is no single approach that is clearly superior in all cases. Many other string matching techniques have been developed that have their individuals strengths. For the purposes of this book, we will use the Jaro-Winkler algorithm because it performs well in matching names due to its bias toward the initial characters, which tend to be more significant. It is also widely supported in the data backends we will use.

Sample Problem

In Chapter 2, we matched two lists of members of the UK House of Commons to explore a proposed correlation between social media presence and reelection. We used exact string matches to establish equivalence between the `Constituency`, `Firstname`, and `Lastname` attributes of the members.

We found 628 true positive matches. But differences between the names meant we didn't find non-exact matches, giving us nine false negatives. Let's see if by using a string similarity metric we can improve our performance. We start by loading the unmatched records that we saved in Chapter 2, as shown in Figure 3-1.

	Constituency	Fullname	Notes	Firstname_w	Lastname_w	Firstname_t	Lastname_t	Flink
0	Burton	Kate Griffiths	Previous incumbent, Andrew Griffiths, did not ...	Kate	Griffiths	Kate	Kniveton	NaN
1	Central Suffolk and North Ipswich	Dan Poulter	Seat held:n	Dan	Poulter	Daniel	Poulter	NaN
2	Newton Abbot	Anne Marie Morris	Seat held:n	Anne	Marie Morris	Anne	Morris	https://facebook.com/annemarie.morris.NA
3	North Antrim	Ian Paisley	Seat held:n	Ian	Paisley	Ian	Paisley Jnr	NaN
4	Slough	Tanmanjeet Dhesi	Seat held:n	Tanmanjeet	Dhesi	Tan	Dhesi	https://facebook.com/tandhesi
5	South Down	Chris Hazzard	Seat held:n	Chris	Hazzard	Christopher	Hazzard	https://facebook.com/chris.hazzard.77
6	South West Norfolk	Liz Truss	Seat held:n	Liz	Truss	Elizabeth	Truss	https://facebook.com/ElizabethTrussSWNorfolk
7	Wealden	Nus Ghani	Seat held:n	Nus	Ghani	Nusrat	Ghani	https://facebook.com/NusGhaniofficial
8	West Dunbartonshire	Martin Docherty-Hughes	Seat held:n	Martin	Docherty-Hughes	Martin	Docherty	https://facebook.com/MartinDochertySNP

Figure 3-1. Unmatched population

Using the `apply` function, we can calculate the Jaro-Winkler similarity metric to compare the first names and last names between the two datasets. We use the Jaro-Winkler algorithm to take advantage of its better performance in matching names:

```
df_w_un['Firstname_jaro'] = df_w_un.apply(
    lambda x: jf.jaro_winkler_similarity(x.Firstname_w, x.Firstname_t), axis=1)

df_w_un['Lastname_jaro'] = df_w_un.apply(
    lambda x: jf.jaro_winkler_similarity(x.Lastname_w, x.Lastname_t), axis=1)
```

We can then apply a threshold of 0.8 on both `Firstname` and `Lastname` attributes, giving us six matches, as shown in Figure 3-2.

```
In [15]: df_mp_un[(df_mp_un['Firstname_jaro'] > 0.8) & (df_mp_un['Lastname_jaro'] > 0.8)]
```

	Constituency	Fullname	Notes	Firstname_x	Lastname_x	Firstname_y	Lastname_y	Flink	Firstname_jaro	Lastname_jaro
1	Central Suffolk and North Ipswich	Dan Poulter	Seat held\n	Dan	Poulter	Daniel	Poulter	NaN	0.883333	1.000000
3	North Antrim	Ian Paisley	Seat held\n	Ian	Paisley	Ian	Paisley Jnr	NaN	1.000000	0.927273
4	Slough	Tanmanjeet Dhesi	Seat held\n	Tanmanjeet	Dhesi	Tan	Dhesi	https://facebook.com/tandhesi	0.836667	1.000000
6	South Down	Chris Hazzard	Seat held\n	Chris	Hazzard	Christopher	Hazzard	https://facebook.com/chris.hazzard.77	0.890909	1.000000
7	Wealden	Nus Ghani	Seat held\n	Nus	Ghani	Nusrat	Ghani	https://facebook.com/NusGhaniofficial	0.883333	1.000000
8	West Dunbartonshire	Martin Docherty-Hughes	Seat held\n	Martin	Docherty-Hughes	Martin	Docherty	https://facebook.com/MartinDochertySNP	1.000000	0.906667

Figure 3-2. Jaro-Winkler match population

Not bad! We have now identified another six of the nine potential matches we previously missed. If we raise the threshold to 0.9 we would have found only two additional matches; if we lowered our threshold to 0.4, all would have matched all nine.

As a reminder, in Chapter 2, we used an exact match on constituency. Then, to identify the unmatched population, we selected those records where either the first name or last name did not match. This allowed us to differentiate between true negatives arising from by-elections and false negatives, where we needed a more flexible matching technique. However, we rarely have a high-cardinality categorical variable like constituency to help us, so we need to consider how we would match these entities on name only.

In this scenario, we can no longer use the simple merge method on exact attribute matches to join our datasets. Instead, we need to manually construct a joint dataset with every possible combination of records and then apply our similarity function to each pair of first name and last name to see which are sufficiently similar. We can then discount those combinations with equivalence scores below a chosen threshold. Clearly, this method can result in a record from the first dataset matching with more than one record from the second.

Full Similarity Comparison

Picking up the cleansed datasets from Chapter 2, we can generate all the record combinations by using the cross-merge function. This generates a row for every name combination between the datasets, producing $650 \times 650 = 422,500$ records:

```
df_w = pd.read_csv('mps_wiki_clean.csv')
df_t = pd.read_csv('mps_they_clean.csv')
cross = df_w.merge(df_t, how='cross',suffixes=('_w', '_t'))
cross.head(n=5)
```

Figure 3-3 shows the first few records in the cross-product dataset.

	Constituency_w	Fullname	Notes	Firstname_w	Lastname_w	Constituency_t	Firstname_t	Lastname_t	Flink
0	Aberavon	Stephen Kinnock	Seat held\n	Stephen	Kinnock	Hackney North and Stoke Newington	Diane	Abbott	https://facebook.com/Dianeabbott
1	Aberavon	Stephen Kinnock	Seat held\n	Stephen	Kinnock	Oldham East and Saddleworth	Debbie	Abrahams	NaN
2	Aberavon	Stephen Kinnock	Seat held\n	Stephen	Kinnock	Selby and Ainsty	Nigel	Adams	https://facebook.com/nigel.adamsmp
3	Aberavon	Stephen Kinnock	Seat held\n	Stephen	Kinnock	Hitchin and Harpenden	Bim	Afolami	NaN
4	Aberavon	Stephen Kinnock	Seat held\n	Stephen	Kinnock	Windsor	Adam	Afriyie	https://facebook.com/adamafriyieofficial

Figure 3-3. Wikipedia, TheyWorkForYou cross-product

We can then calculate the Jaro-Winkler similarity metrics for both first name and last name on each row. Applying a threshold of 0.8 allows us to determine for each row whether these values approximately match:

```
cross['Firstname_jaro'] = cross.apply(lambda x: True if
    jf.jaro_winkler_similarity(x.Firstname_w, x.Firstname_t);0.8
    else False, axis=1)

cross['Lastname_jaro'] = cross.apply(lambda x: True if
    jf.jaro_winkler_similarity(x.Lastname_w, x.Lastname_t);0.8
    else False, axis=1)
```

We can then select records where both the Firstname and Lastname attributes are approximately equivalent to our prospective matches. We can check whether these are correct by using the Constituency attribute to verify our results. We know that when the constituency doesn't match we aren't referring to the same member of Parliament.

So let's see how many true positive matches we have now:

```
tp = cross[(cross['Firstname_jaro'] & cross['Lastname_jaro']) &
    (cross['Constituency_w']==cross['Constituency_t'])]

len(tp)
634
```

These true positives include the 628 exact matches from Chapter 2 plus the 6 approximate matches we identified earlier. But let's see how many false positives we have picked up where the name attributes are approximately equivalent but the Constituency doesn't match:

```
fp = cross[(cross['Firstname_jaro'] & cross['Lastname_jaro']) &
    (cross['Constituency_w']!=cross['Constituency_t'])]

len(fp)
19
```

Let's take a look at a few of these 19 mismatching records in Figure 3-4.

	Constituency_w	Fullname	Notes	Firstname_w	Lastname_w	Constituency_t	Firstname_t	Lastname_t	Flink
40659	Blyth Valley	Ian Levy	Previous incumbent, Ronnie Campbell, did not s...	Ian	Levy	Wansbeck	Ian	Lavery	https://facebook.com/IanLaveryMP
72718	Cardiff Central	Jo Stevens	Seat held'n	Jo	Stevens	Carlisle	John	Stevenson	https://facebook.com/JohnStevensonCarlisle
73245	Cardiff North	Anna McMorrin	Seat held'n	Anna	McMorrin	Newton Abbot	Anne	Morris	https://facebook.com/annemarie.morris.NA
75316	Carlisle	John Stevenson	Seat held'n	John	Stevenson	Cardiff Central	Jo	Stevens	https://facebook.com/JoStevensLabour
76340	Carmarthen West and South Pembrokeshire	Simon Hart	Seat held'n	Simon	Hart	North Dorset	Simon	Hoare	https://facebook.com/simonhoarenorthdorset

Figure 3-4. Full match false positives

We can see that there is a similarity between these names although they do not refer to the same individual. These mismatches are the price we pay for adopting a similarity match to maximize our number of true positives.

We can also examine the candidates we rejected by examining where the constituency matches but either the first name or last name doesn't. We have to inspect these manually to determine whether they are true or false negatives.

```
fntn = cross[(~cross['Firstname_jaro'] | ~cross['Lastname_jaro']) &
    (cross['Constituency_w']==cross['Constituency_t'])]

len(fntn)
16
```

Figure 3-5 shows these 16 negative match records.

Within the 16 negatives we can see the 13 by-election constituencies we declared as true negatives in Chapter 2, plus 3 false negatives in the constituencies of Burton, South West Norfolk, and Newton Abbot, where the names are sufficiently different that their Jaro-Winkler match score falls below our 0.8 threshold.

```
In [25]: fntn
Out[25]:
```

	Constituency_w	Fullname	Notes	Firstname_w	Lastname_w	Constituency_t	Firstname_t	Lastname_t		Flink
3100	Airdrie and Shotts	Neil Gray	Seat held\n	Neil	Gray	Airdrie and Shotts	Anum	Qaisar		NaN
19211	Batley and Spen	Tracy Brabin	Seat held\n	Tracy	Brabin	Batley and Spen	Kim	Leadbeater		NaN
30812	Birmingham Erdington	Jack Dromey	Seat held\n	Jack	Dromey	Birmingham Erdington	Paulette	Hamilton		NaN
64899	Burton	Kate Griffiths	Previous incumbent, Andrew Griffiths, did not ...	Kate	Griffiths	Burton	Kate	Kniveton		NaN
84750	Chesham and Amersham	Cheryl Gillan	Seat held\n	Cheryl	Gillan	Chesham and Amersham	Sarah	Green		NaN
90506	City of Chester	Chris Matheson	Seat held\n	Chris	Matheson	City of Chester	Samantha	Dixon		NaN
174650	Hartlepool	Mike Hill	Seat held\n	Mike	Hill	Hartlepool	Jill	Mortimer		NaN
255245	Newton Abbot	Anne Marie Morris	Seat held\n	Anne	Marie Morris	Newton Abbot	Anne	Morris	https://facebook.com/annemarie.morris.NA	
266943	North Shropshire	Owen Paterson	Seat held\n	Owen	Paterson	North Shropshire	Helen	Morgan		NaN
281023	Old Bexley and Sidcup	James Brokenshire	Seat held\n	James	Brokenshire	Old Bexley and Sidcup	Louie	French		NaN
342502	South West Norfolk	Liz Truss	Seat held\n	Liz	Truss	South West Norfolk	Elizabeth	Truss	https://facebook.com/ElizabethTrussSWNorfolk	
345356	Southend West	David Amess	Seat held\n	David	Amess	Southend West	Anna	Firth		NaN
361373	Stretford and Urmston	Kate Green	Seat held\n	Kate	Green	Stretford and Urmston	Andrew	Western		NaN
373312	Tiverton and Honiton	Neil Parish	Seat held\n	Neil	Parish	Tiverton and Honiton	Richard	Foord		NaN
384521	Wakefield	Imran Ahmad Khan	Defeated incumbent, Mary Creagh\n	Imran	Ahmad Khan	Wakefield	Simon	Lightwood		NaN
401187	West Lancashire	Rosie Cooper	Seat held\n	Rosie	Cooper	West Lancashire	Ashley	Dalton		NaN

Figure 3-5. Full match true and false negatives

Measuring Performance

Now let's consider how our performance compares to the exact-only matching in Chapter 2:

$$Recall = \frac{TP}{(TP + FN)} = \frac{634}{(634 + 3)} \approx 99.2\%$$

$$Precision = \frac{TP}{(TP + FP)} = \frac{634}{(634 + 19)} \approx 97\%$$

$$Accuracy = \frac{(TP + TN)}{(TP + TN + FP + FN)} = \frac{(634 + 13)}{(634 + 13 + 19 + 3)} \approx 96.7\%$$

We can see in Table 3-2 that introducing a similarity threshold instead of demanding an exact match has improved our recall. In other words, we have missed fewer true matches, but at the expense of declaring a few incorrect matches, which reduces our precision and our overall accuracy.

Table 3-2. Exact versus approximate matching performance

	Exact match	Approximate match
Precision	100%	97%
Recall	98.6%	99.2%
Accuracy	98.5%	96.7%

In this simple example, we set a threshold of 0.8 for both first name and last name, and we demanded that both attributes exceed this score for use to declare a match. This assigned the same importance to both attributes, but perhaps a match on first name isn't as strong as a match on last name?

Let's have a look at how much repetition we see in both first names and last names in the Wikipedia dataset:

```
df_w['Firstname'].value_counts().mean()
1.8950437317784257

df_w['Lastname'].value_counts().mean()
1.1545293072824157
```

In this dataset, each `Firstname` is found, on average, 1.89 times versus 1.15 times for each `Lastname`. Therefore we could say that a `Lastname` match is 64% (1.89/1.15) more differentiating than a `Firstname` match. In the next chapter, we will examine how we can use probabilistic techniques to weight the importance of each attribute and combine these to produce an overall match confidence score.

Summary

In this chapter, we have explored how to use approximate matching techniques to assess the degree of equivalence between two attributes. We examined several algorithms for approximate text matching and set an equivalence threshold above which we declared a match.

We saw how approximate matching can help us to find true positive matches we would otherwise miss but at the price of some false positives that we had to discount manually. We saw how the equivalence threshold we set affects this trade-off in performance.

Finally, we considered whether we should give equal weight to matching attributes that have different levels of uniqueness when we are evaluating whether two records refer to the same entity.

CHAPTER 4

Probabilistic Matching

In Chapter 3, we explored how to use approximate matching techniques to measure the degree of similarity between attribute values. We set a threshold above which we declared equivalence and then combined these matching features, with equal weight, to conclude that two records referred to the same entity when both were a match. We evaluated our performance against exact matches only.

In this chapter, we will examine how to use probability-based techniques to calculate the optimum weighting for each equivalent attribute in calculating the likelihood of an overall entity match. This probability-based approach allows us to declare a match when the most statistically significant attributes are equivalent (either exact or approximate) but those with less significance are insufficiently similar. It also allows us to grade our confidence in the declaration of a match and apply appropriate match thresholds. The model that will be introduced in this section is known as the Fellegi-Sunter (FS) model.

We will also introduce a probabilistic entity resolution framework, Splink, that we will use to help us calculate these metrics and resolve our entities together.

Sample Problem

Let's return to our exact match results from the end of Chapter 2. Opening the *Chapter4.ipynb* notebook we reload the standardized datasets from the Wikipedia and TheyWorkForYou websites. As in Chapter 3, we start by calculating the Cartesian, or cross, product of the two datasets as:

```
cross = df_w.merge(df_t, how='cross', suffixes=('_w', '_t'))
```

This gives us our total population of $650 \times 650 = 422{,}500$ record pairs—a pair for every name combination between the Wikipedia and TheyWorkForYou datasets.

Throughout this chapter, we will be using exact matches between the `Firstname`, `Lastname`, and `Constituency` fields of each of these record pairs multiple times. Thus, it's more efficient to calculate these matches once and store them as additional feature columns:

```
cross['Fmatch']= (cross['Firstname_w']==cross['Firstname_t'])
cross['Lmatch']= (cross['Lastname_w']==cross['Lastname_t'])
cross['Cmatch']= (cross['Constituency_w']==cross['Constituency_t'])
```

We also calculate the total number of matching columns, which we will use later:

```
cross['Tmatch'] =
    sum([cross['Fmatch'],cross['Lmatch'],cross['Cmatch']])
```

Based on our exploration of the data in Chapter 2, we know that within our total population of 422,500 combinations we have 637 record pairs that have an exact match on constituency and either first name or last name. This is our `match` population:

```
match = cross[cross['Cmatch'] & (cross['Fmatch'] |
    cross['Lmatch'])]
```

The remainder, our `notmatch` population, is extracted as the inverse:

```
notmatch = cross[(~cross['Cmatch']) | (~cross['Fmatch'] &
    ~cross['Lmatch'])]
```

These combinations are summarized in Table 4-1.

Table 4-1. Match and not match combinations

Match/not match population	Constituency match	First name match	Last name match
Not match	No	No	No
Not match	No	No	Yes
Not match	No	Yes	No
Not match	No	Yes	Yes
Not match	Yes	No	No
Match	Yes	No	Yes
Match	Yes	Yes	No
Match	Yes	Yes	Yes

We will now examine how well first name and last name equivalence, both individually and together, can predict whether an individual record belongs in either the `match` or `notmatch` population.

Single Attribute Match Probability

Let's begin by considering whether first name equivalence alone is a good indicator that two entities within a record pair refer to the same person. We will examine both the `match` and `notmatch` populations and establish, within each of those subsets, how many first names match and how many do not.

Naming Convention

As we work through various subsets of these populations, it's helpful to adopt a standard naming convention so that we can see at a glance how each population of records was selected. As we select records we add the selection criteria to the population name, right to left, e.g., `first_match` should be read as first selecting those records that are part of the `match` population and within that subset of the population further selecting only those rows where the first names are equivalent.

First Name Match Probability

Starting with the `match` population we can select those records where the first names are equivalent to give us our `first_match` population:

```
first_match = match[match['Fmatch']]
```

```
len(first_match)
632
```

Repeating this for the three other combinations of match/not match, and first name equivalence or not, we can draw up a population map, as shown in Figure 4-1.

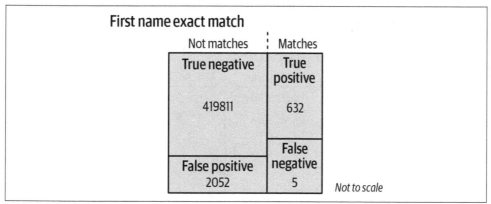

Figure 4-1. First name population map

Therefore, based on first name equivalence only, we have:

$$True\ positive\ matches\ (TP) = 632$$

$$False\ positive\ matches\ (FP) = 2052$$

$$True\ negative\ matches\ (TN) = 419811$$

$$False\ negative\ matches\ (FN) = 5$$

Now we can calculate some probability values. First, the probability that a record pair whose first names are equivalent is actually a true positive match can be calculated as the number of pairs within the match population whose first names match divided by the number of pairs whose first names match across both the match and notmatch populations:

$$prob\_match\_first = \frac{len(first\_match)}{(len(first\_match) + len(first\_notmatch))} = \frac{632}{(632 + 2052)} \approx 0.2355$$

From this we can see that, at only about 23%, first name equivalence alone isn't a great predictor of a match between two records. This value is a conditional probability, that is, it is the probability of a true positive match conditional on the first name being a match. This can be written as:

$$P(match\,|\,first)$$

where the pipe character (|) is read as "given that."

Last Name Match Probability

Applying the same calculations to the last name, we can draw a second population map, as shown in Figure 4-2.

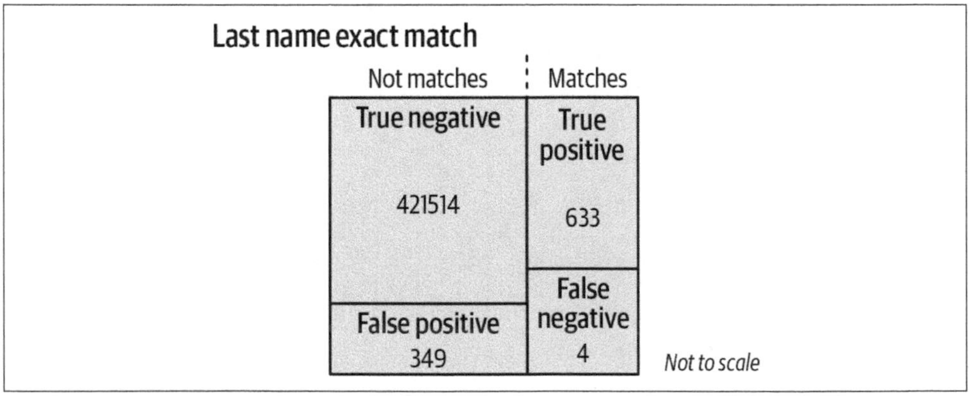

Last name exact match

	Not matches	Matches
	True negative 421514	True positive 633
	False positive 349	False negative 4

Not to scale

Figure 4-2. Last name population map

As for first name, the probability that a pair of records whose last names are equivalent is actually a match can be calculated as the number of pairs within the `match` population whose last names match divided by the number of pairs whose last names match across both the `match` and `notmatch` populations.

$$prob\_match\_last = \frac{len(last\_match)}{(len(last\_match) + len(last\_notmatch))} = \frac{633}{(633 + 349)} \approx 0.6446$$

For these records last name equivalence is clearly a better predictor of a true match than first name, which instinctively makes sense.

Again, this can be written as:

$$P(match \mid last)$$

Multiple Attribute Match Probability

Now if we consider both first name and last name equivalence we can further subdivide our population map. Starting with our first name map and further subdividing each first name category into last name equivalence, and not, we can view our population as shown in Figure 4-3.

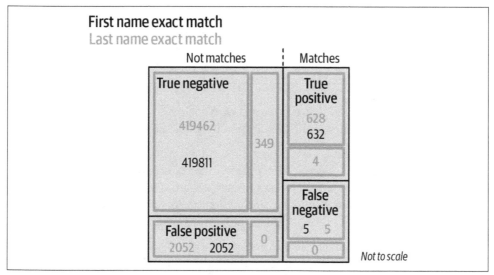

Figure 4-3. First name, last name population map

Extending our calculation to both first name and last name exact matches, we can calculate the probability of a true positive match given both first name and last name equivalence as:

$$prob\_match\_last\_first = \frac{len(last\_first\_match)}{(len(last\_first\_match) + len(last\_first\_notmatch)}$$
$$= \frac{628}{(628 + 0)} = 1.0$$

If the first name matches but last name doesn't, what is the probability that it's a match?

$$prob\_match\_notlast\_first = \frac{len(notlast\_first\_match)}{(len(notlast\_first\_match) + len(notlast\_first\_notmatch))}$$
$$= \frac{4}{(4 + 2052)} \approx 0.0019$$

If the first name doesn't match but the last name does, what is the probability that it's a match?

$$prob\_match\_last\_notfirst = \frac{len(last\_notfirst\_match)}{(len(last\_notfirst\_match) + len(last\_notfirst\_notmatch))}$$
$$= \frac{5}{(5 + 349)} \approx 0.0141$$

As we expected, if either first name or last name isn't an exact match, then the probability of a true positive match is low, but a last name match gives us more confidence than a first name one.

If neither first name nor last name matches, the probability that it is a match is:

$$prob\_match\_notlast\_notfirst =$$
$$\frac{len(notlast\_notfirst\_match)}{(len(notlast\_notfirst\_match) + len(notlast\_notfirst\_notmatch))} = \frac{0}{(0 + 419462)} = 0$$

This is not surprising given that we defined true positive matches as records with an exact match on constituency and either first name or last name.

In conclusion, we can use these probabilities to inform our decision making on whether we are likely to have a true positive match or not. In this example, we would place more weight on a last name match than a first name one. This is an improvement on our method in Chapter 3, where we gave them the same weighting (and required them both to be equivalent) to declare a match.

But wait, we have a problem. In the preceding example, we started with a known population of matches that we used to compute the probabilities that first name and last name equivalence equate to a match. However, in most situations we don't have a known match population; otherwise we wouldn't need to perform matching in the first place! How do we overcome this? To do so, we need to reframe our calculation a little and then employ some clever estimation techniques.

Probabilistic Models

In the previous section, we learned that some attributes are more informative than others; that is, they have more predictive power to help us decide whether a match is likely to be correct. In this section, we examine how to calculate these contributions and how to combine them to assess the overall likelihood of a match.

We start with a little statistical theory (using first name equivalence as an example) before we generalize to model what we can deploy at scale.

Bayes' Theorem

Bayes' theorem, named after Thomas Bayes, states that the conditional probability of an event, based on the occurrence of another event, is equal to the probability of the second event given the first event, multiplied by the probability of the first event.

Consider the probability that two records chosen at random are a true positive match, P(match), multiplied by the probability that within those matches the first names match, P (first|match):

$$P(first|match) \times P(match)$$

Equally, we could calculate the same value in the reverse order, starting with the probability that the first name matches, P(first) multiplied by the probability that records within this population are a true positive match:

$$P(match|first) \times P(first)$$

Equating these probabilities, we have:

$$P(match|first) \times P(first) = P(first|match) \times P(match)$$

Rearranging we can calculate:

$$P(match|first) = \frac{P(first|match) \times P(match)}{P(first)}$$

We can calculate P(first) as the sum of the probabilities across both the match and notmatch populations:

$$P(first) = (P(first|match) \times P(match)$$
$$+ P(first|notmatch) \times P(notmatch))$$

Substituting in the preceding equation, we have:

$$P(match|first) = \frac{P(first|match) \times P(match)}{P(first|match) \times P(match) + P(first|notmatch) \times P(notmatch)}$$

Alternatively, we can rearrange this as:

$$P(match|first) = 1 - \left(1 + \frac{P(first|match)}{P(first|notmatch)} \times \frac{P(match)}{P(notmatch)}\right)^{-1}$$

If we can estimate the values in this equation, we can determine the probability that if a first name is equivalent, then the record pair really is a match.

Let's examine these values in a little more detail, simplifying the notation as we go along.

m Value

The conditional probability that an attribute will be equivalent within the overall match population is known as the *m value*. Using our Firstname example, we can denote this as:

$$m_f = P(first|match)$$

In a perfect dataset, all the first names within the match population would be exactly equivalent and the *m* value would be 1. This value can therefore be thought of as a measure of data quality, i.e., how much variability there is in how an attribute has been captured across the datasets. A higher value indicates a better-quality attribute.

u Value

The conditional probability that an attribute will be equivalent within the overall notmatch population is known as the *u value*. Again, using our Firstname example, we can denote this as:

$$u_f = P(first|notmatch)$$

This value reflects how much commonality there is in this attribute across the datasets. A lower value indicates a less common, more distinguishing attribute that, if found to be equivalent in a particular case, would lead us to question whether it belongs in the notmatch population and is really a match. Conversely, a higher *u* value tells us that this particular attribute is not as valuable for determining overall matches.

A good example of u value is a month of birth attribute, which, assuming the population is equally distributed across the year, will have a u value of $\frac{1}{12}$.

Lambda (λ) Value

The *lambda value*, λ, also known as the prior, is the probability that two randomly chosen records match.

$$\lambda = P(match)$$

In contrast with the m and u values, the λ value is a record-level value not associated with any particular attribute. This value is a measure of how much duplication there is in the dataset overall and is the starting point for our probability calculations.

The inverse, the likelihood that two randomly chosen records are not a match, can be written as follows:

$$1 - \lambda = P(notmatch)$$

Bayes Factor

Substituting these compact notations can result in the following:

$$P(match|first) = 1 - \left(1 + \frac{m_f}{u_f} \times \frac{\lambda}{(1-\lambda)}\right)^{-1}$$

The ratio $\frac{m_f}{u_f}$ is also known as the *Bayes factor*, in this case of the `Firstname` parameter. The Bayes factor, as a combination of both the m and u values, gives a measure of the significance we should attach to the fact that the `Firstname` values were equivalent.

Fellegi-Sunter Model

The *Fellegi-Sunter model*, named after Ivan P. Fellegi and Alan B. Sunter,[1] describes how we can extend our simple Bayesian approach, combining the contribution of multiple attributes, to calculate the overall likelihood of a match. It relies on the simplifying assumption of conditional independence between attributes, also known as *naive Bayes*.

---

1 The original paper is available online (*https://oreil.ly/gcfWx*).

Using the FS model, we can combine the Bayes factors associated with each attribute in our record by simply multiplying them together. Taking our Firstname example and extending it to consider when the Lastname is also equivalent we have:

$$P(match\,|\,last\,|\,first) = 1 - \left(1 + \frac{m_f}{u_f} \times \frac{m_l}{u_l} \times \frac{\lambda}{(1-\lambda)}\right)^{-1}$$

When an attribute isn't equivalent, the Bayes factor is calculated as the inverse, $\frac{(1-m_l)}{(1-u_l)}$. Therefore when the Firstname is equivalent but the Lastname is not, we calculate the probability of an overall match as:

$$P(match\,|\,notlast\,|\,first) = 1 - \left(1 + \frac{m_f}{u_f} \times \frac{(1-m_l)}{(1-u_l)} \times \frac{\lambda}{(1-\lambda)}\right)^{-1}$$

Once we can calculate the m and u values for each attribute, and the λ value for the overall dataset, we can easily calculate the probabilities for each record pair. We simply determine the equivalence of each attribute (either exact or approximate as appropriate), select the appropriate Bayes factors, and multiply them together using the preceding formula to calculate the overall probability for that record pair.

For our simple example, our Bayes factors are therefore calculated as shown in Table 4-2.

Table 4-2. Firstname, Lastname match factor calculations

Firstname equivalence	Lastname equivalence	Firstname Bayes factor	Lastname Bayes factor	Combined Bayes factor
No	No	$\frac{(1-m_f)}{(1-u_f)}$	$\frac{(1-m_l)}{(1-u_l)}$	$\frac{(1-m_f)}{(1-u_f)} \times \frac{(1-m_l)}{(1-u_l)}$
No	Yes	$\frac{(1-m_f)}{(1-u_f)}$	$\frac{m_l}{u_l}$	$\frac{(1-m_f)}{(1-u_f)} \times \frac{m_l}{u_l}$
Yes	No	$\frac{m_f}{u_f}$	$\frac{(1-m_l)}{(1-u_l)}$	$\frac{m_f}{u_f} \times \frac{(1-m_l)}{(1-u_l)}$
Yes	Yes	$\frac{m_f}{u_f}$	$\frac{m_l}{u_l}$	$\frac{m_f}{u_f} \times \frac{m_l}{u_l}$

Match Weight

To make overall match calculations more intuitive, the logarithm of the Bayes factors is sometimes used so that they can be added together rather than multiplied. In this way it is easy to visualize the relative contribution of each attribute to the overall score.

For our simple first name and last name equivalence example, the logarithmic match weight might be calculated (using base 2) as:

$$MatchWeight = log_2\frac{m_f}{u_f} + log_2\frac{m_l}{u_l} + log_2\frac{\lambda}{(1-\lambda)}$$

We can calculate probability from the match weight as:

$$Probability = 1 - \left(1 + 2^{MatchWeight}\right)^{-1}$$

Now that we understand how to combine our individual attribute probabilities, or match weights, together let's consider how to estimate our λ value and our m and u values for each attribute when we don't have a known match population. One technique that we can use is called the *expectation-maximization (EM) algorithm* (*https://oreil.ly/kvWD3*).

Expectation-Maximization Algorithm

The expectation-maximization algorithm uses an iterative approach to approximating the λ and m and u values. Let's see a simplified form of this in action applied to our sample problem.

Iteration 1

For the first iteration we make the opening assumption that record pairs where the majority of the feature columns are equivalent are matches:

```
it1_match = cross[cross['Tmatch']>=2]
it1_notmatch = cross[cross['Tmatch']<2]

len(it1_match)
637
```

This gives us a pseudo match population, it1_match, of 637 records. In addition to the 628 perfect matches we found in Chapter 2, we also have 9 matches where either Firstname or Lastname (but not both) doesn't match, as we see in Figure 4-4:

```
it1_match[~it1_match['Fmatch'] | ~it1_match['Lmatch']]
    [['Constituency_w','Firstname_w','Firstname_t',
        'Lastname_w','Lastname_t']]
```

	Constituency_w	Firstname_w	Firstname_t	Lastname_w	Lastname_t
64699	Burton	Kate	Kate	Griffiths	Kniveton
79794	Central Suffolk and North Ipswich	Dan	Daniel	Poulter	Poulter
255245	Newton Abbot	Anne	Anne	Marie Morris	Morris
256580	North Antrim	Ian	Ian	Paisley	Paisley Jnr
326453	Slough	Tanmanjeet	Tan	Dhesi	Dhesi
331778	South Down	Chris	Christopher	Hazzard	Hazzard
342502	South West Norfolk	Liz	Elizabeth	Truss	Truss
393480	Wealden	Nus	Nusrat	Ghani	Ghani
399909	West Dunbartonshire	Martin	Martin	Docherty-Hughes	Docherty

Figure 4-4. Expectation-maximization iteration 1 additional matches

Our initial λ value is therefore:

$$\lambda_1 = \frac{637}{650 \times 650} \approx 0.0015$$

$$(1 - \lambda_1) = (1 - 0.0015) \approx 0.9985$$

Our initial prior match weight is therefore $log_2 \frac{\lambda_1}{(1 - \lambda_1)} \approx -9.371$.

As a starting point, it's therefore extremely unlikely that two records are a match. Now let's calculate our *m* and *u* values so that we can update our probability on a per-record basis.

As we have a pseudo match and notmatch population, it's straightforward to calculate our *m* and *u* values as the proportion of each population with an equivalent attribute. For Firstname, Lastname, and Constituency we use:

```
mfi1 = len(it1_match[it1_match['Fmatch']])/len(it1_match)
mli1 = len(it1_match[it1_match['Lmatch']])/len(it1_match)
mci1 = len(it1_match[it1_match['Cmatch']])/len(it1_match)

ufi1 = len(it1_notmatch[it1_notmatch['Fmatch']])/len(it1_notmatch)
uli1 = len(it1_notmatch[it1_notmatch['Lmatch']])/len(it1_notmatch)
uci1 = len(it1_notmatch[it1_notmatch['Cmatch']])/len(it1_notmatch)
```

Table 4-3 shows these values and the resulting match weight values per attribute.

Table 4-3. Iteration 1 m and u values

Attribute	*m* value	*u* value	Match Bayes factor	Match weight	Not match Bayes factor	Not match weight
Firstname	0.9921	0.0049	203.97	7.67	0.0079	−6.98
Lastname	0.9937	0.0008	1201.19	10.23	0.0063	−7.31
Constituency	1.0	0.0	∞	∞	0	−∞

There are no record pairs where the constituency is equivalent in the notmatch population, so its *u* value is 0 and therefore its match weight is mathematically infinity and its notmatch weight is negative infinity.

Now we can use these values in the Fellegi-Sunter model to calculate the match probability for every record pair in the full population. We use a helper function to calculate these probabilities based on the values of the Constituency, Firstname, and Lastname match features:

```
def match_prb(Fmatch,Lmatch,Cmatch,mf1,ml1,mc1,uf1,ul1,uc1, lmbda):
    if (Fmatch==1):
        mf = mf1
        uf = uf1
    else:
        mf = (1-mf1)
        uf = (1-uf1)
    if (Lmatch==1):
        ml = ml1
        ul = ul1
    else:
        ml = (1-ml1)
        ul = (1-ul1)
    if (Cmatch==1):
        mc = mc1
        uc = uc1
    else:
        mc = (1-mc1)
        uc = (1-uc1)
    prob = (lmbda * ml * mf * mc) / (lmbda * ml * mf * mc +
        (1-lmbda) * ul * uf * uc)
    return(prob)
```

We apply this function to the whole population with:

```
cross['prob'] = cross.apply(lambda x: match_prb(
    x.Fmatch,x.Lmatch,x.Cmatch,
    mfi1,mli1,mci1,
    ufi1,uli1,uci1,
    lmbda), axis=1)
```

Once we've calculated these values we can iterate again, resegmenting our population into match and notmatch populations based on the calculated match probabilities.

Iteration 2

For illustration purposes, we use an overall match probability of greater than 0.99 to define our new assumed match population and assign any record with an equal or lower probability to our notmatch population:

```
it2_match = cross[cross['prob']>0.99]
it2_notmatch = cross[cross['prob']<=0.99]

len(it2_match)
633
```

Applying this 0.99 threshold gives us a slightly reduced match population of 633. Let's see why. If we select the records just below the threshold we can see:

```
it2_notmatch[it2_notmatch['prob']>0.9]
    [['Constituency_w', 'Lastname_w','Lastname_t','prob']]
```

	Constituency_w	Lastname_w	Lastname_t	prob
64699	Burton	Griffiths	Kniveton	0.984329
255245	Newton Abbot	Marie Morris	Morris	0.984329
256580	North Antrim	Paisley	Paisley Jnr	0.984329
399909	West Dunbartonshire	Docherty-Hughes	Docherty	0.984329

Figure 4-5. Iteration 2 records with below-the-line match thresholds

As we see in Figure 4-5, if the Lastname isn't equivalent, the new match probability falls just below our 0.99 threshold. Using these new match and notmatch populations we can revise our λ, m, and u values and iterate again, recalculating the match probabilities for each record pair.

In this case, our λ doesn't materially change:

$$\lambda_2 = \frac{633}{650 \times 650} \approx 0.0015$$

Only the Lastname values change slightly, as shown in Table 4-4.

Table 4-4. Iteration 2 m and u values

Attribute	*m* value	*u* value	Match Bayes factor	Match weight	Not match Bayes factor	Not match weight
Firstname	0.9921	0.0049	203.97	7.67	0.0079	−6.98
Lastname	1.0	0.0008	1208.79	10.24	0	−∞
Constituency	1.0	0.0	∞	∞	0	−∞

Iteration 3

In this simple example, this next iteration doesn't change the match population, which remains at 633, because the EM algorithm has already converged.

This gives us our final parameter values of:

$$\lambda \approx 0.0015$$
$$m_f = P(first|match) \approx 0.9921$$
$$m_l = P(last|match) \approx 1.0$$
$$m_c = P(constituency|match) \approx 1.0$$
$$u_f = P(first|notmatch) \approx 0.0049$$
$$u_l = P(last|notmatch) \approx 0.0008$$
$$u_c = P(constituency|notmatch) \approx 0$$

This instinctively feels right. We know that a match will always have an equivalent constituency and either first name or last name will match, with last name slightly more likely to be equivalent than first name (five out of nine versus four out of nine in the preceding sample).

Similarly, we know the constituency will never be the same in a notmatch record pair and it's very unlikely that either the first name or last name will accidentally match either (with first name slightly more likely).

We can turn these estimated values into match probabilities using the equations in the previous section:

$$P(match|last|first) = 1 - \left(1 + \frac{m_f}{u_f} \times \frac{m_l}{u_l} \times \frac{\lambda}{(1-\lambda)}\right)^{-1} = 1.0$$

$$P(match|notlast|first) = 1 - \left(1 + \frac{m_f}{u_f} \times \frac{(1-m_l)}{(1-u_l)} \times \frac{\lambda}{(1-\lambda)}\right)^{-1} \approx 0.0019$$

$$P(match|notfirst|last) = 1 - \left(1 + \frac{(1-m_f)}{(1-u_f)} \times \frac{m_l}{u_l} \times \frac{\lambda}{(1-\lambda)}\right)^{-1} \approx 0.0141$$

$$P(match|notfirst|notlast) = 1 - \left(1 + \frac{(1-m_f)}{(1-u_f)} \times \frac{(1-m_l)}{(1-u_l)} \times \frac{\lambda}{(1-\lambda)}\right)^{-1} = 0$$

As expected, these probabilities match the values we calculated using the probability maps in Figure 4-3 when we knew the match and notmatch population upfront.

In conclusion, we are now able to estimate match probabilities for all the different permutations of attribute equivalence without having to know the `match` population in advance. This probabilistic approach is both powerful and scalable to large datasets with multiple attributes. To help us apply these techniques more easily, we introduce a performant and easy-to-use open source library, Splink, in the next section.

Introducing Splink

Splink is a Python package for probabilistic entity resolution. Splink implements the Fellegi-Sunter model and includes a variety of interactive outputs to help users understand models and diagnose linkage problems.

Splink supports a number of backends to perform the matching calculations. To begin with, we will use DuckDB, an in-process SQL database management system, that we can run locally on our laptop.

Configuring Splink

To import Splink into our notebook, we use:

```
import splink
```

Splink requires a unique ID column in each dataset, so we need to create these by copying their respective DataFrame indexes:

```
df_w['unique_id'] = df_w.index
df_t['unique_id'] = df_t.index
```

Splink also needs the same columns to be present in both datasets. Therefore, we need to create blank columns where these are present in only one set of records and then remove unnecessary columns:

```
df_w['Flink'] = None
df_t['Notes'] = None

df_w = df_w[['Firstname','Lastname','Constituency','Flink','Notes',
    'unique_id']]
df_t = df_t[['Firstname','Lastname','Constituency','Flink','Notes',
    'unique_id']]
```

Our next step is to configure Splink settings:

```
from splink.duckdb.linker import DuckDBLinker
from splink.duckdb import comparison_library as cl

settings = {
    "link_type": "link_only", "comparisons": [
        cl.exact_match("Firstname"),
        cl.exact_match("Lastname"),
        cl.exact_match("Constituency"),
    ],
}
linker = DuckDBLinker([df_w, df_t], settings)
```

Splink supports both deduplication of records within a single dataset and linking between one or more separate datasets. Here we set link_type to link_only to tell Splink that we want only to match, not deduplicate, between our two datasets. We also tell Splink the comparisons we wish to use, in this case exact matches across our three attributes. Lastly, we instantiate the linker with these settings and our source DataFrames.

To help us understand our datasets, Splink provides a visualization of the distribution of the columns to be matched:

```
linker.profile_columns(['Firstname','Lastname','Constituency'])
```

The graphs we see in Figure 4-6 show us the combined population across both datasets.

Starting with distribution of first names we can see from the bottom right of the graph that, within the population of 352 distinct names, approximately 35% occur only twice, most probably once in each dataset. Then, moving right to left, we see a gradual increase in frequency to the most popular name, with 32 occurrences. Looking at the top 10 values by value count we see that John is the most popular name, followed by Andrew, David, etc. This tells us that Firstname is a reasonable attribute to match on, but used alone, it will result in some false positives.

For last name the pattern is more stark, with a larger population of 574 distinct names, of which nearly 80% occur only twice. Looking at the top 10 values, the most common last names, Smith and Jones, occur 18 times, almost half as common as the most popular first name. As expected, this tells us that Lastname is a richer attribute than Firstname and therefore its equivalence is a better predictor of matching entities.

As expected, constituencies are uniquely paired across the two datasets, so all values appear exactly twice.

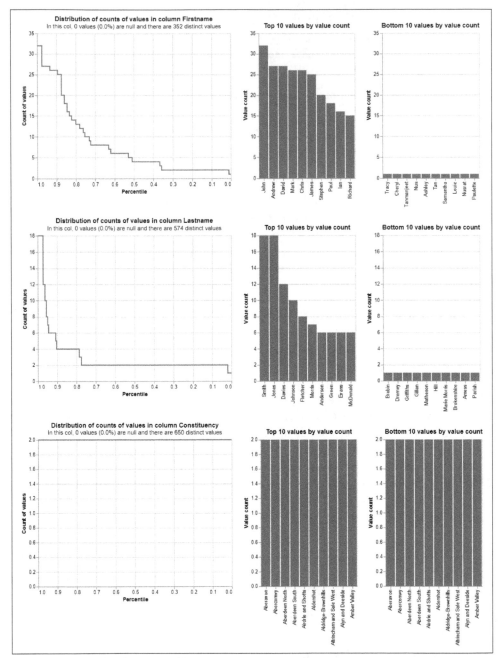

Figure 4-6. Splink column profiles

For the purposes of this simple example, we're going to ask Splink to calculate all the parameters of the model using the expectation-maximization algorithm we introduced earlier. The initial True parameter tells Splink to compare all the records across both datasets without blocking (we'll see this in the next chapter). We also tell Splink to recalculate the u values at each iteration by setting fix_u_probabilities to False. Setting the fix_probability_two_random_records_match to False means the λ value (the overall match probability between the two datasets) will be recalculated at each iteration. Finally, we tell Splink to use the updated λ value when calculating probabilities for record pairs.:

```
em_session = linker.estimate_parameters_using_expectation_maximisation(
    'True',
    fix_u_probabilities=False,
    fix_probability_two_random_records_match=False,
    populate_probability_two_random_records_match_from_trained_values
      =True)
```

Splink Performance

The EM model converges after three iterations. Splink produces an interactive chart showing the iterative progression of the relative match weights values:

```
em_session.match_weights_interactive_history_chart()
```

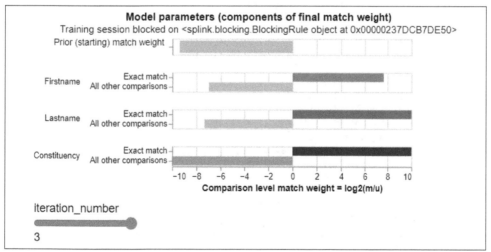

Figure 4-7. Splink match weights

Figure 4-7 shows the final match weights that Splink has calculated after the third iteration. First, we have the prior (starting) match weight, which is a measure of how likely it is that two records chosen at random match. If you hover over the match weight bars you can see the calculated match weight value together with the underlying m and u parameters. These are calculated as follows:

$$Prior(starting)\ match\ weight = log_2\frac{\lambda}{(1-\lambda)} \approx -9.38$$

$$First\ name\ match\ weight\ (exact\ match) = log_2\frac{m_f}{u_f} \approx 7.67$$

$$First\ name\ match\ weight\ (not\ exact\ match) = log_2\frac{(1-m_f)}{(1-u_f)} \approx -6.98$$

$$Last\ name\ match\ weight\ (exact\ match) = log_2\frac{m_l}{u_l} \approx 10.23$$

$$Last\ name\ match\ weight\ (not\ exact\ match) = log_2\frac{(1-m_l)}{(1-u_l)} \approx -7.32$$

$$Constituency\ match\ weight\ (exact\ match) = log_2\frac{m_c}{u_c} \approx 14.98$$

For illustration purposes, Splink approximates the Constituency not exact match weight as negative infinity and displays it in a different color. This is because there are no cases where the Firstname and Lastname attributes match but the Constituency does not.

We can see the discrete values Splink has calculated using:

```
linker.save_settings_to_json("Chapter4_Splink_Settings.json",
    overwrite=True)
{'link_type': 'link_only',
 'comparisons': [{'output_column_name': 'Firstname',
    'comparison_levels': [{'sql_condition': '"Firstname_l" IS NULL OR
        "Firstname_r" IS NULL',
     'label_for_charts': 'Null',
     'is_null_level': True},
   {'sql_condition': '"Firstname_l" = "Firstname_r"',
     'label_for_charts': 'Exact match',
     'm_probability': 0.992118804074688,
     'u_probability': 0.0048664290128404288},
   {'sql_condition': 'ELSE',
     'label_for_charts': 'All other comparisons',
     'm_probability': 0.007881195925311958,
     'u_probability': 0.9951357098715956}],
    'comparison_description': 'Exact match vs. anything else'},
  {'output_column_name': 'Lastname',
    'comparison_levels': [{'sql_condition': '"Lastname_l" IS NULL OR
        "Lastname_r" IS NULL',
     'label_for_charts': 'Null',
     'is_null_level': True},
   {'sql_condition': '"Lastname_l" = "Lastname_r"',
     'label_for_charts': 'Exact match',
     'm_probability': 0.9937726043638647,
     'u_probability': 0.00082730840955421},
   {'sql_condition': 'ELSE',
```

```
          'label_for_charts': 'All other comparisons',
          'm_probability': 0.006227395636135347,
          'u_probability': 0.9991726915904457}],
        'comparison_description': 'Exact match vs. anything else'},
      {'output_column_name': 'Constituency',
        'comparison_levels': [{'sql_condition': '"Constituency_l" IS NULL OR
            "Constituency_r" IS NULL',
          'label for charts': 'Null',
          'is_null_level': True},
        {'sql_condition': '"Constituency_l" = "Constituency_r"',
          'label_for_charts': 'Exact match',
          'm_probability': 0.9999999403661186,
          'u_probability': 3.092071473132138e-05},
        {'sql_condition': 'ELSE',
          'label_for_charts': 'All other comparisons',
          'm_probability': 5.963388147277392e-08,
          'u_probability': 0.9999690792852688}],
        'comparison_description': 'Exact match vs. anything else'}],
    'retain_intermediate_calculation_columns': True,
    'retain_matching_columns': True,
    'sql_dialect': 'duckdb',
    'linker_uid': 'adm20und',
    'probability_two_random_records_match': 0.0015075875293170335}
```

The *m* and *u* probabilities match those we calculated manually using the expectation-maximization algorithm earlier in the chapter.

Finally, as before, we apply a threshold match probability and select the record pair above the threshold:

```
pres = linker.predict(threshold_match_probability =
    0.99).as_pandas_dataframe()

len(pres)
633
```

Analysis of these predictions shows that all 633 are true positives, leaving the 13 by-election true negatives and 4 false negatives. We can view the 4 false negatives with:

```
m_outer = match.merge(
    pres,
    left_on=['Constituency_t'],
    right_on=['Constituency_l'],
    how='outer')

m_outer[m_outer['Constituency_t']!=m_outer['Constituency_l']]
    [['Constituency_w','Lastname_w','Lastname_t']]
```

The output, shown in Figure 4-8, shows that the mismatch on Lastname is the reason these entities fall below the match threshold.

	Constituency_w	Lastname_w	Lastname_t
96	Burton	Griffiths	Kniveton
386	Newton Abbot	Marie Morris	Morris
388	North Antrim	Paisley	Paisley Jnr
603	West Dunbartonshire	Docherty-Hughes	Docherty

Figure 4-8. Splink below the threshold due to Lastname mismatch

In comparison to the unweighted results in Chapter 3, Splink declares a match for "Liz Truss" versus "Elizabeth Truss," but does not match "Anne Marie Morris" to "Anne Morris," nor "Martin Docherty-Hughes" to "Martin Docherty." This is because it is more heavily influenced by a mismatch on Lastname, which is statistically a better negative predictor, than a mismatch on Firstname.

Summary

To recap, we took two sets of records and combined them into a composite dataset containing every record pair combination. We then computed exact match features between equivalent fields and then combined those features, weighted according to how often they occurred in both the matching and nonmatching populations, to determine the overall likelihood of a match.

We saw how to use probability theory to calculate the match weights using the iterative expectation-maximization algorithm when we don't have known match populations.

Finally, we introduced the probabilistic entity resolution framework Splink, which greatly simplified the calculations when combining multiple attributes and helped us visualize and understand our match results.

Now that we have worked through a small-scale example, we will apply the techniques of approximate and probabilistic matching on a larger scale.

CHAPTER 5

Record Blocking

In Chapter 4, we introduced probabilistic matching techniques to allow us to combine exact equivalence on individual attributes into a weighted composite score. That score allowed us to calculate the overall probability that two records refer to the same entity.

So far we have sought to resolve only small-scale datasets where we could exhaustively compare every record with every other to find all possible matches. However, in most entity resolution scenarios, we will be dealing with larger datasets where this approach isn't practical or affordable.

In this chapter we will introduce record blocking to reduce the number of permutations we need to consider while minimizing the likelihood of missing a true positive match. We will leverage the Splink framework, introduced in the last chapter, to apply the Fellegi-Sunter model and use the expectation-maximization algorithm to estimate the model parameters.

Lastly, we will consider how to measure our matching performance over this larger dataset.

Sample Problem

In previous chapters, we considered the challenge of resolving entities across two datasets containing information about members of the UK House of Commons. In this chapter, we extend this resolution challenge to a much larger dataset containing a list of the persons with significant control of registered UK companies.

In the UK, Companies House is an executive agency sponsored by the Department for Business and Trade. It incorporates and dissolves limited companies, registering company information and making it available to the public.

When registering a UK limited company, there is an obligation to declare who owns or controls a company. These entities are known as persons with significant control (PSCs); they're sometimes called "beneficial owners." Companies House provides a downloadable data snapshot containing the full list of PSCs.

For this exercise, we will attempt to resolve the entities listed in this dataset with the list of members of Parliament we acquired from Wikipedia. This will show us which MPs may be PSC of UK companies.

Data Acquisition

In this example, we will reuse the same Wikipedia source data on MPs returned at the 2019 UK general election that we examined in previous chapters. However, to allow us to match against a much larger dataset, without generating an unmanageable number of false positives, we need to enrich our initial data with additional attributes. Specifically, we will seek to augment our dataset with date of birth information, extracted from the individual wiki page associated with each of the MPs, to help strengthen the quality of our matches.

We will also download the most recent snapshot of the PSC data published by Companies House and then normalize and filter that dataset down to the attributes we need for matching.

Wikipedia Data

To create our enriched Wikipedia dataset, we select the MPs from the wiki page as we did in Chapter 2; however, this time we also extract the Wikipedia link to each individual MP and append this as an additional column in our DataFrame.

```
url = "https://en.wikipedia.org/wiki/
      List_of_MPs_elected_in_the_2019_United_Kingdom_general_election"

website_page = requests.get(url).textsoup =
    BeautifulSoup(website_page,'html.parser')
tables = soup.find_all('table')

for table in tables:
   if 'Member returned' in table.text:
       headers = [header.text.strip() for header in table.find_all('th')]
       headers = headers[:5]
       dfrows = []
       table_rows = table.find_all('tr')
       for row in table_rows:
          td = row.find_all('td')
          dfrow = [row.text for row in td if row.text!='\n']
          tdlink = row.find_all("td", {"data-sort-value" : True})
          for element in tdlink:
              for link in element.select("a[title]"):
```

```
                        urltail = link['href']
                        url = f'https://en.wikipedia.org{urltail}'
                dfrow.append(url)
                dfrows.append(dfrow)
            headers.append('Wikilink')
        df_w = pd.DataFrame()
```

We can now follow these links and extract the date of birth information, if present, from the web page Infobox. As before, we can use the Beautiful Soup html parser to find and extract the attribute we need or return a default null value. The apply method allows us to apply this function to each row in the Wikipedia dataset, creating a new column entitled Birthday:

```
def get_bday(url):
    wiki_page = requests.get(url).text
    soup = BeautifulSoup(wiki_page,'html.parser')
    bday = ''
    bdayelement = soup.select_one("span[class='bday']")
    if bdayelement is not None:
        bday = bdayelement.text
        return(bday)

df_w['Birthday'] = df_w.apply(lambda x: get_bday(x.Wikilink), axis=1)
```

UK Companies House Data

Companies House publishes a snapshot of PSC data in JSON format. It is made available both as a single ZIP file and as multiple ZIP files for ease of downloading. Extracting each partial ZIP file in turn allows us to normalize the JSON structure that we concatenate into a composite DataFrame of the attributes we need for matching plus the associated unique company number:

```
url = "http://download.companieshouse.gov.uk/en_pscdata.html"

>df_psctotal = pd.DataFrame()
with requests.Session() as req:
    r = req.get(url)
    soup = BeautifulSoup(r.content, 'html.parser')
    snapshots = [f"{url[:38]}{item['href']}" for item in soup.select(
        "a[href*='psc-snapshot']")]
    for snapshot in snapshots:
        print(snapshot)
        response = requests.get(snapshot).content zipsnapshot =
            zipfile.ZipFile(io.BytesIO(response))
        tempfile = zipsnapshot.extract(zipsnapshot.namelist()[0])
        df_psc = pd.json_normalize(pd.Series(open(tempfile,
            encoding="utf8").readlines()).apply(json.loads))

        must_cols =  ['company_number',
                      'data.name_elements.surname',
                      'data.name_elements.middle_name',
```

```
                    'data.name_elements.forename',
                    'data.date_of_birth.month',
                    'data.date_of_birth.year',
                    'data.name_elements.title',
                    'data.nationality']
        all_cols =list(set(df_psc.columns).union(must_cols))

>       df_psc=df_psc.reindex(columns=sorted(all_cols))
        df_psc = df_psc.dropna(subset=['company_number',
                    'data.name_elements.surname',
                    'data.name_elements.forename',
                    'data.date_of_birth.month',
                    'data.date_of_birth.year'])
    df_psc = df_psc[must_cols]
    df_psctotal = pd.concat([df_psctotal, df_psc],
        ignore_index=True)
```

Data Standardization

Now that we have the raw data we need, we standardize the attributes and column names across the two datasets. As we will be using the Splink framework, we also add a unique ID column.

Wikipedia Data

To standardize the date-enriched Wikipedia data, we convert the date column into month and year integers. As in Chapter 2, we extract Firstname and Lastname attributes. We also add a unique ID column and a blank company number column to match the equivalent field in the Companies House data. Finally, we retain only the columns we need:

```
df_w = df_w.dropna()
df_w['Year'] =
    pd.to_datetime(df_w['Birthday']).dt.year.astype('int64')
df_w['Month'] =
    pd.to_datetime(df_w['Birthday']).dt.month.astype('int64')

df_w = df_w.rename(columns={ 'Member returned' : 'Fullname'})
df_w['Fullname'] = df_w['Fullname'].str.rstrip("\n")
df_w['Fullname'] = df_w['Fullname'].str.lstrip("\n")
df_w['Firstname'] = df_w['Fullname'].str.split().str[0]
df_w['Lastname'] = df_w['Fullname'].astype(str).apply(lambda x:
    ' '.join(x.split()[1:]))

df_w['unique_id'] = df_w.index
df_w["company_number"] = np.nan

df_w=df_w[['Firstname','Lastname','Month','Year','unique_id',
    'company_number']]
```

UK Companies House Data

To standardize the UK Companies House data, we first drop any rows with missing year or month date of birth columns as we won't be able to match these records. As with the Wikipedia data, we standardize the column names, generate the unique ID, and retain the matching subset:

```
df_psc = df_psc.dropna(subset=['data.date_of_birth.year',
                               'data.date_of_birth.month'])

df_psc['Year'] = df_psc['data.date_of_birth.year'].astype('int64')
df_psc['Month'] = df_psc['data.date_of_birth.month'].astype('int64')
df_psc['Firstname']=df_psc['data.name_elements.forename']
df_psc['Lastname']=df_psc['data.name_elements.surname']
df_psc['unique_id'] = df_psc.index

df_psc = df_psc[['Lastname','Firstname','company_number',
    'Year','Month','unique_id']]
```

Let's look at a few rows (with Firstnames and Lastnames sanitized), as shown in Figure 5-1.

	Lastname	Firstname	company_number	Year	Month	unique_id
0			09145694	1977	2	0
1			08581893	1947	9	1
2			08581893	1965	6	2
3			01605766	1960	10	3
4			10259080	1976	9	4

Figure 5-1. Example rows of UK Companies House persons with significant control data

Record Blocking and Attribute Comparison

Now that we have consistent data, we can configure our matching process. Before we do, it's worth taking a look at the size of the challenge. We have 650 MP records and our standardized PSC data has more than 10 million records. If we were to consider all permutations, we would have approximately 6 billion comparisons to make.

Performing a simple join on records with matching Month and Year values, we can see the size of the intersection is approximately 11 million records:

```
df_mp = df_w.merge(df_psc, on=['Year','Month'],
    suffixes=('_w','_psc'))

len(df_mp)
11135080
```

A simple exact match on all four attributes yields 266 potential matches:

```
df_result = df_w.merge(df_psc, on= ['Lastname','Firstname','Year','Month'],
    suffixes=('_w', '_psc'))
```

```
df_result
```

A sanitized sample of these simple join matches is shown in Figure 5-2.

	Firstname	Lastname	Month	Year	unique_id_w	company_number_w	company_number_psc	unique_id_psc
0			10	1968	1	NaN	04569484	1231207
1			10	1968	1	NaN	06975241	4255185
2			10	1976	5	NaN	08204196	621989
3			11	1967	6	NaN	02715837	3297081
4			5	1967	7	NaN	07484717	6535599
...	...	...	...	...	...	...	...	...
261			1	1982	638	NaN	10791041	3538484
262			1	1982	638	NaN	12131090	5999020
263			6	1971	642	NaN	07355501	234243
264			2	1963	644	NaN	13636383	8245001
265			11	1970	646	NaN	08569809	4113711

266 rows × 8 columns

Figure 5-2. Simple join on `Lastname`, `Firstname`, `Year`, and `Month`

Record Blocking with Splink

To reduce the number of record combinations we need to consider, Splink allows us to configure blocking rules. These rules determine which record pairs are evaluated to determine whether they refer to the same entity. Clearly, considering only a subset of the population creates a risk of missing true matches, it's important to select rules that minimize this while at the same time reducing the volume as much as possible.

Splink allows us to create composite rules, essentially OR statements, where if any of the conditions are met, then the combination is selected for further comparison. However, in this example we'll use only a single blocking rule that selects only records with matching year and month of birth:

```
from splink.duckdb.linker import DuckDBLinker
from splink.duckdb import comparison_library as cl
settings = {
    "link_type": "link_only",
    "blocking_rules_to_generate_predictions":
        ["l.Year = r.Year and l.Month = r.Month"],
    "comparisons": [
        cl.jaro_winkler_at_thresholds("Firstname", [0.9]),
        cl.jaro_winkler_at_thresholds("Lastname", [0.9]),
        cl.exact_match("Month"),
        cl.exact_match("Year", term_frequency_adjustments=True),
        ],
        "additional_columns_to_retain": ["company_number"]
}
```

Attribute Comparison

For the record comparisons that are produced by the blocking rules, we will determine whether they refer to the same person by using a combination of approximate
matches scores on first name and last name and exact matches on month and
year. Because we are comparing names, we use the Jaro-Winkler algorithm from
Chapter 3.

We can configure Splink with a set of minimum threshold values that together
segment the population; Splink will add an exact match segment and a default zero
match segment for those attribute pairs that score beneath the minimum value provided. In this case, we will just use a single threshold of 0.9 to illustrate the process,
giving us three segments for each component of the name. Each segment is evaluated
as a separate attribute for the purposes of calculating the overall match probability of
the record pair.

Now that we have our settings, let's instantiate our linker and profile the matching
columns:

```
linker = DuckDBLinker([df_w, df_psc], settings,
    input_table_aliases = ["df_w", "df_psc"])
linker.profile_columns(["Firstname","Lastname","Month","Year"],
    top_n=10, bottom_n=5)
```

You can see the results in Figure 5-3.

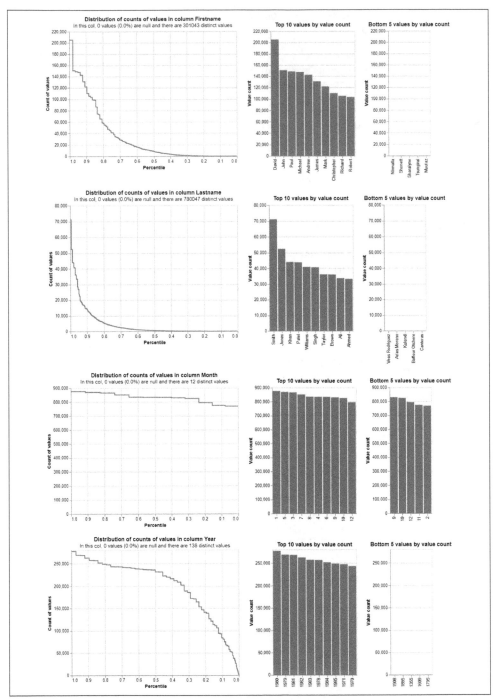

Figure 5-3. First name, last name, month, and year distributions

We can see that we have some common first names and last names with a long tail of less frequent values. For month of birth, the values are fairly regularly distributed but for year, we see some years are more likely than others. We can take this frequency distribution into account in our matching process by setting:

```
term_frequency_adjustments=True
```

Each year value will be considered separately for the purposes of calculating match probabilities; thus a match on an unpopular year will be weighted more highly than a match on a more frequently observed value.

As we did in Chapter 4, we could use the expectation-maximization algorithm to determine the m and u values, that is, the match and not match probabilities, for each attribute segment. By default, these calculations consider the full population prior to applying the blocking rules.

To estimate the u values, Splink takes a slightly different approach by taking random pairwise record comparisons, assuming they do not match, and computing how often these coincidences occur. Since the probability of two random records being a match (representing the same entity) is usually very low, this approach generates good estimates of the u values. An additional benefit of this approach is that if the u probabilities are correct, it "anchors" the EM estimation procedure and greatly improves the chance of it converging to a global, rather than a local, minimum. To apply this approach, we need to make sure our random population is sufficiently large to be representative of the full range of possible combinations:

```
linker.estimate_u_using_random_sampling(max_pairs=1e7)
```

Splink allows us to set blocking rules for estimating the match probabilities. Here the attribute parameters for each segment are estimated on the subset of the population according to the first condition and then the process is repeated for the subset selected by the second condition. Since the attributes included in the blocking condition cannot themselves be estimated, it is essential that the conditions overlap, allowing each attribute to be evaluated under at least one condition.

Random Sample

Note that the expectation-maximization method selects records at random, so you can expect some variation from the calculated parameters in this book if you are following along.

In this example, we block on equivalent last name and month, allowing us to estimate first name and year segment probabilities, and then we repeat with the opposite combination. This way each attribute segment is evaluated at least once:

```
linker.estimate_parameters_using_expectation_maximisation
   ("l.Lastname = r.Lastname and l.Month = r.Month",
      fix_u_probabilities=False)
linker.estimate_parameters_using_expectation_maximisation
   ("l.Firstname = r.Firstname and l.Year = r.Year",
      fix_u_probabilities=False)
```

We can examine the resulting match weights using:

```
linker.match_weights_chart()
```

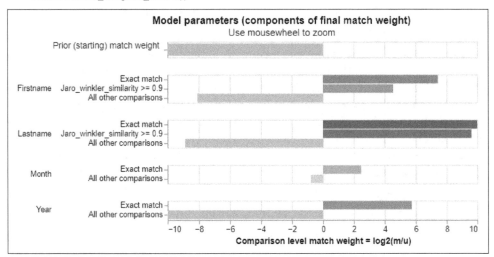

Figure 5-4. Model parameters

In Figure 5-4, we can see a strongly negative prior (starting) match weight with positive weights for each attribute exact match and for approximate matches on Firstname and Lastname:

```
linker.m_u_parameters_chart()
```

In Figure 5-5, we can see the proportion of matching and nonmatching record comparisons that the expectation maximization algorithm calculates for each segment.

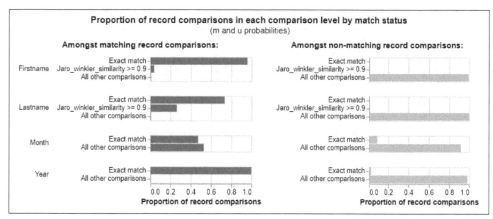

Figure 5-5. Proportion of record comparisons

Match Classification

Now that we have a trained model with optimized match parameters for each attribute, we can predict whether the record pairs that aren't blocked refer to the same entity. In this example, we set an overall threshold match probability at 0.99:

```
results = linker.predict(threshold_match_probability=0.99)
pres = results.as_pandas_dataframe()
```

We then join the prediction results to the PSC dataset by unique ID so that we can pick up the company number that the matched entity is associated with.

Then we rename our output columns and retain only the ones we need:

```
pres = pres.rename(columns={"Firstname_l": "Firstname_psc",
                            "Lastname_l": "Lastname_psc",
                            "Firstname_r":"Firstname_w",
                            "Lastname_r":"Lastname_w",
                            "company_number_l":"company_number"})
pres = pres[['match_weight','match_probability',
            'Firstname_psc','Firstname_w',
            'Lastname_psc','Lastname_w','company_number']]
```

This gives us 346 predicted matches, both exact and approximate, as shown in Figure 5-6 (with the PSC first names and last names sanitized).

	match_weight	match_probability	Firstname_psc	Firstname_w	Lastname_psc	Lastname_w	company_number
0	12.772967	0.999857		Peter		Gibson	03142623
1	13.024241	0.999880		Alister		Jack	SC436811
2	12.900714	0.999869		Jonathan		Djanogly	08280731
3	12.889262	0.999868		Anthony		Mangnall	09915512
4	13.122115	0.999888		Graham		Stuart	SC525993
...	...	...	...	...	...	...	...
341	13.122115	0.999888		Graham		Stuart	02099304
342	12.747826	0.999855		Peter		Kyle	09855158
343	12.747255	0.999855		Sarah		Jones	06469073
344	10.206447	0.999154		Jeff		Smith	13311041
345	13.323386	0.999902		Geoffrey		Cox	13328052

346 rows × 7 columns

Figure 5-6. Exact matches on Lastname and Firstname

If we remove the exact matches, we can examine the additional approximate matches to see how well our probabilistic approach has performed. This is shown in Figure 5-7 (with the PSC first names and last names sanitized):

```
pres[(pres['Lastname_psc']!=pres['Lastname_w']) |
     (pres['Firstname_psc']!=pres['Firstname_w'])]
```

	match_weight	match_probability	Firstname_psc	Firstname_w	Lastname_psc	Lastname_w	company_number
5	11.668858	0.999693		Richard		Thomson	10609747
6	13.514815	0.999915		John		McDonnell	05350064
7	11.100448	0.999545		Jamie		Stone	SC042883
8	9.983912	0.999013		Jeff		Smith	09530115
15	9.983912	0.999013		Jeff		Smith	13311041
...	...	...	...	...	...	...	...
319	11.917547	0.999742		Mark		Garnier	06540656
322	8.767288	0.997710		John		Glen	12254404
327	9.681758	0.998784		Theo		Clarke	08140289
331	8.767288	0.997710		John		Glen	14106498
339	11.719844	0.999704		Anthony		Browne	12521856

80 rows × 7 columns

Figure 5-7. Approximate matches—nonexact Firstname or Lastname

Examining the results, shown in Table 5-1, we can see several candidates that may be true positive matches.

Table 5-1. Approximate matches—manual comparison

match_weight	match_proba bility	First name_psc	First name_w	Last name_psc	Last name_w	company_ number
13.51481459	0.999914572	John	John	Mcdonnell	McDonnell	5350064
11.66885836	0.999692963	Stephen	Stephen	Mcpartland	McPartland	7572556
11.50728191	0.999656589	James	James	Heappey Mp	Heappey	5074477
9.637598832	0.998746141	Matt	Matthew	Hancock	Hancock	11571107
13.51481459	0.999914572	John	John	Mcdonnell	McDonnell	4662034
9.320995827	0.998438931	Siobhan	Siobhan	Mcdonagh	McDonagh	246884
11.46050878	0.999645277	Alison	Alison	Mcgovern	McGovern	10929919
9.57364719	0.998689384	Jessica	Jess	Phillips	Phillips	560074
12.14926274	0.999779904	Grahame	Grahame	Morris Mp	Morris	13523499
11.66885836	0.999692963	Stephen	Stephen	Mcpartland	McPartland	9165947
13.51481459	0.999914572	John	John	Mcdonnell	McDonnell	6496912
11.62463457	0.999683409	Anna	Anna	Mcmorrin	McMorrin	9965110

Despite our initial data standardization, we can see that we have inconsistent capitalization on last name, and we also have a couple of PSC records where the last name is appended with "Mp." This is frequently the case with entity resolution problems—we often have to iterate several times, refining our data standardization as we learn more about our dataset.

Measuring Performance

If we assume that all the exact matches and the approximate matches in Table 5-1 are true positive matches, then we can calculate our precision metrics as:

$$True\,positive\,matches\,(FP) = 266 + 12 = 278$$

$$False\,positive\,matches\,(FP) = 80 - 12 = 68$$

$$Precision = \frac{TP}{(TP + FP)} = \frac{278}{(278 + 68)} \approx 80\,\%$$

Without manual verification, we don't definitively know which of our notmatch population are true or false negatives, and therefore we cannot calculate recall or overall accuracy metrics.

Summary

In this chapter, we used approximate matching within a probabilistic framework to identify members of Parliament who may have significant control over UK companies.

We saw how blocking can be used to reduce the number of record pairs we need to evaluate to a practical size without unacceptably increasing the risk that we miss some important potential matches.

We saw how important data standardization is to optimizing performance and how getting the best performance in entity resolution is often an iterative process.

CHAPTER 6

Company Matching

In Chapter 5, we examined the challenge of resolving a larger set of individual entities, matching on name and date of birth. In this chapter, we consider another typical scenario, resolving organization entities so that we can get a more complete picture of their business.

We could perhaps use the date of incorporation of the organization as a discriminator, similar to the way we used date of birth to help identify unique individuals. However, this incorporation date information is not typically included in organization datasets; it is much more common for a company to be identified by its registered address.

Therefore, in this chapter, we will use company address information, along with company names, to identify likely matches. We will then consider how to evaluate a new record for matches against the original data sources without having to undertake a time-consuming retrain of the model.

Sample Problem

In this chapter, we will resolve a list of company names that is published by the UK Maritime and Coastguard Agency (MCA) against basic organization details published in the Companies House register. This problem illustrates some of the challenges of identifying unique references to the same company, simply based on name and address data.

UK Companies House provides a free downloadable data snapshot containing basic company data of live companies on the register. This data complements the "person with significant control" data we used in Chapter 5.

The MCA publishes a list of recruitment and placement agencies approved under Regulation 1.4 of the Maritime Labour Convention (MLC) 2006.[1]

Data Acquisition

To acquire the datasets, we use the same approach we used in Chapter 5. The MCA data, published as a single comma-separated values (CSV) file, is downloaded and ingested into a DataFrame. The Companies House snapshot data is downloaded as ZIP files, and the extracted JSON structure is then parsed into a DataFrame. Unwanted columns are then removed and the snapshot DataFrames are concatenated into a single composite DataFrame. Both raw datasets are then stored locally as CSV files for ease of reloading.

The code is available as *Chapter6.ipynb* in the GitHub repository (*https://git hub.com/mshearer0/HandsOnEntityResolution*).

Data Standardization

To match the MCA company list to the Companies House organization dataset, we need to standardize the name and address data into the same format. We have seen how to cleanse names. Addresses, however, pose more of a challenge. Even within reasonably consistent data from same source, we often see considerable variation in address format and content.

For example, consider the first three records in the MCA list, as shown in Table 6-1.

Table 6-1. MCA sample addresses

Address attribute
48 Charlotte Street, London, W1T 2NS
4th Floor, 105 George Street, Glasgow, G2 1PB
Unit 16, Beaverbank Business Park EH7 4HG

We can see the first address is made up of three comma-separated elements, the second record by four elements, and the third again by only two. In each case, the postcode is contained in the final element, but in the third record, it is grouped with part of the address itself. The building number is present in either the first element or the second element.

---

1 MLC 2006 regulates the operation of seafarer recruitment and placement services to inform seafarers seeking employment on ships flying flags other than those of their own countries.

To view a histogram distribution of the number of address elements in the MCA list we can use:

```
import matplotlib.pyplot as plt
plt.hist(df_m.apply(lambda row: len(row['ADDRESS & CONTACT
    DETAILS'].split(',')), axis=1).tolist())
```

This gives us the distribution chart presented in Figure 6-1.

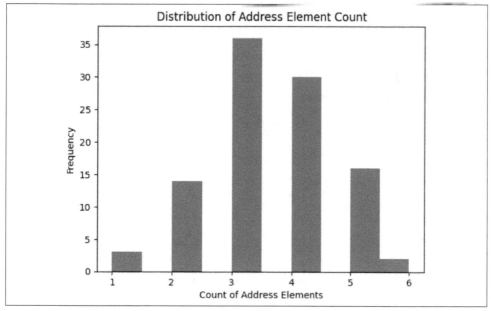

Figure 6-1. MCA address element count

This lack of consistency makes parsing addresses consistently into the same discrete elements for matching quite difficult. Therefore, for this example, we will use just exact postcode matches to compare addresses. More advanced parsing and matching techniques, such as natural language processing and geocoding, are discussed in Chapter 11.

Companies House Data

In many jurisdictions companies are required to declare the nature of their incorporation at the end of their name, for example, adding "Limited" or "Ltd" if they are constituted as a limited liability company. These variable suffixes may not always be present, so standardization is challenging.

To ensure a mismatch doesn't unduly negatively interfere with the matching process, it is advisable to separate these lower-value terms from the name record as part of the standardization process. This will remove the chance of missing a potential match due to inconsistencies in suffix format, at the risk of declaring a false positive match between, say, a public limited company and a limited company with similar names.

In addition to removing incorporation suffixes, it can also be helpful to remove common terms that don't differentiate between companies and whose inclusion would otherwise exaggerate the similarity of our name matches.

Although we choose to remove these terms, or *stopwords*, from the company name attribute, they do still contain some value that may be useful when the decision to declare a match is in the balance.

The following helper function strips these stopwords, returning the cleansed company name and the removed terms:

```
def strip_stopwords(raw_name):
    company_stopwords = { 'LIMITED', 'LTD', 'SERVICES', 'COMPANY',
        'GROUP', 'PROPERTIES', 'CONSULTING', 'HOLDINGS', 'UK',
        'TRADING', 'LTD.', 'PLC','LLP' }
    name_without_stopwords = []
    stopwords = []
    for raw_name_part in raw_name.split():
        if raw_name_part in company_stopwords:
            stopwords.append(raw_name_part)
        else:
            name_without_stopwords.append(raw_name_part)
    return(' '.join(name_without_stopwords),
           ' '.join(stopwords))
```

We can apply this function to the Company House data using:

```
df_c[['CompanyName','Stopwords']] =  pd.DataFrame(
    zip(*df_c['CompanyName'].apply(strip_stopwords))).T
```

The * operator unzips the series of tuples (containing CompanyName and Stopwords) returned by the helper function. We assemble these value lists into a two-row DataFrame that we then transpose to columns so that we can add as new attributes. This approach is efficient as we only have to create a new DataFrame once as opposed to per row.

Because we already have a discrete column containing a discrete postcode, all that remains is to standardize the column name:

```
df_c = df_c.rename(columns={"RegAddress.PostCode": "Postcode"})
```

Maritime and Coastguard Agency Data

To standardize the MCA company name, we first convert the name to uppercase:

```
df_m['CompanyName'] = df_m['COMPANY'].str.upper()
```

We also remove the stopwords and then we need to extract the postcode from the address field. A convenient way to do this is to use a *regular expression*.

Regular Expression

A regular expression is a sequence of characters that specifies a match pattern in text. Usually such patterns are used by string-searching algorithms for "find" or "find and replace" operations on strings, or for input validation.

A UK postcode is made up of two parts. The first part compromises one or two capital letters followed by a single digit and then either a single digit or a single capital letter. After a space, the second part begins with a single digit followed by two capital letters (excluding CIKMOV). This can be encoded as:

```
r'([A-Z]{1,2}[0-9][A-Z0-9]? [0-9][ABD-HJLNP-UW-Z]{2})'
```

We can construct a helper function to find, extract, and return a matching pattern of characters or return a null value if not found:

```
import re
def extract_postcode(address):
    pattern = re.compile(r'([A-Z]{1,2}[0-9][A-Z0-9]?
        [0-9][ABD-HJLNP-UW-Z]{2})')
    postcode = pattern.search(address)
    if(postcode is not None):
    return postcode.group()
        else:
    return None
```

As before, we can apply this function to every row:

```
df_m['Postcode'] = df_m.apply(lambda row:
    extract_postcode(row['ADDRESS & CONTACT DETAILS']), axis=1)
```

Record Blocking and Attribute Comparison

As in the previous chapter, we will use the Splink tool to perform the matching process. Let's consider the settings that will allow us to do this.

First, we can expect organizations with matching postcodes to be reasonable match candidates and similarly those with exactly equivalent names. We can use these conditions as our blocking rules, only calculating predictions when either condition is fulfilled:

```
"blocking_rules_to_generate_predictions":
    ["l.Postcode = r.Postcode",
     "l.CompanyName = r.CompanyName", ],
```

Splink provides a handy visualization for us to see the volume of record pairs that will pass the blocking rules. As expected, there are a significant number of postcode matches and very few exact name matches, as shown in Figure 6-2.

```
linker.cumulative_num_comparisons_from_blocking_rules_chart()
```

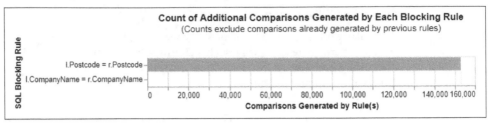

Figure 6-2. Blocking rule comparisons

Within that subset of potential combinations, we evaluate the similarity of the selected pair of CompanyName entries in four segments:

- Exact match
- Jaro-Winkler score of >0.9
- Jaro-Winkler score between 0.8 and 0.9
- Jaro-Winkler score of <0.8

We also evaluate the stopwords in a similar manner.

The corresponding Splink settings are:

```
"comparisons": [
    cl.jaro_winkler_at_thresholds("CompanyName", [0.9,0.8]),
    cl.jaro_winkler_at_thresholds("Stopwords",[0.9]),
],
```

Of course, those pairs that pass the blocking rule as exact name equivalents will be evaluated as exact matches, whereas those with only a postcode match will be evaluated as candidates for both exact and approximate name matching.

Before we can apply the blocking rules and calculate our match probabilities, we need to train our model. The Cartesian product of the two DataFrames is >500 million pairwise combinations, so we train the u value using random sampling over 50 million target rows to have a reasonable sample:

```
linker.estimate_u_using_random_sampling(max_pairs=5e7)
```

As in Chapter 5, we use the expectation-maximization algorithm to estimate the m values. Here we block on only matching postcodes because the tiny relative proportion of name matches has no beneficial effect on the parameter estimation:

```
linker.estimate_parameters_using_expectation_maximisation(
    "l.Postcode = r.Postcode")
```

We can display the proportion of records in each segment that the trained model observes using:

```
linker.match_weights_chart()
```

The record comparison chart, seen in Figure 6-3, shows a strong differentiation on CompanyName similarity between matching and nonmatching records. For the stopwords, there is only a marked differentiation between the approximately matching records at similarity threshold equal to or greater than 0.9, but not exact.

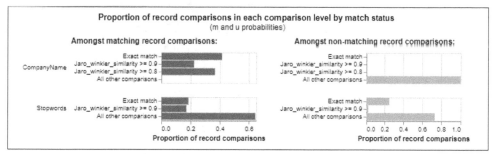

Figure 6-3. Proportion of record comparisons by match status

As expected, the parameters chart (as shown in Figure 6-4) shows that exact and approximate CompanyName matches have strong match weights:

```
linker.m_u_parameters_chart()
```

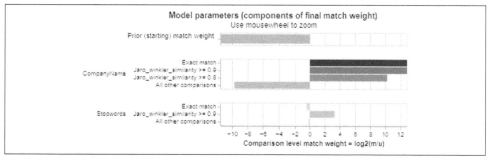

Figure 6-4. Model parameters

Match Classification

In this example, we expect to find a match for each of the MCA organizations in the Companies House dataset, so we set a low match threshold of 0.05 to make sure we surface as many potential matches as possible:

```
df_pred = linker.predict(threshold_match_probability=0.05)
    .as_pandas_dataframe()
```

To identify the MCA entities where we failed to find at least one match, we can merge our predictions with the MCA dataset by unique_id and then select those results with a null match weight:

```
results = df_m.merge(df_pred,left_on=['unique_id'], right_on=
    ['unique_id_r'],how='left', suffixes=('_m', '_p'))
results[results['match_weight'].isnull()]
```

As shown in Figure 6-5, this produces 11 records for which we didn't find any match.

	Postcode	CompanyName	unique_id
25	HU10 7WG	CP MARINE	17
27	M50 2EQ	CREW BOARD	19
33	CT16 3PX	DFDS SEAWAYS BV	25
94	FY4 6GU	MR MIM WORLD OF ENTERTAINMENT	54
96	KT23 4HN	NEPTUNE MANNING	56
97	EN1 3TF	NEW ENTERTAINMENT AND SERVICE	57
112	DT4 9LY	ROBSON CREW RECRUITMENT	67
143	PO6 3TD	STR (TRADING AS NAVIS LTD)	77
149	AB10 1TT	TEAM RECRUITMENT	83
152	BN7 2NN	THE CREW ACADEMY (INC "THE CREW HUNTER" BRAND)	86
161	BH15 4QE	VANTAGE YACHT RECRUITMENT	93

Figure 6-5. Unmatched records

At the time of writing, a manual search of Companies House reveals that 7 of these 11 entities have candidate matches, but these candidates do not have exact matching postcodes or names and so were filtered out by our blocking rules. Two of these entities have candidates with exact match postcodes but significantly different names and so fall below our approximate similarity threshold. Finally, the two remaining candidates have been dissolved and so are not included in our live companies snapshot.

A convenient way to examine the predicted matches and the contribution that an attribute makes to the overall match score is to draw a match weight waterfall chart:

```
linker.waterfall_chart(df_pred.to_dict(orient="records"))
```

In the example given in Figure 6-6, we can see that the prior match weight, a measure of the likelihood that two records chosen at random refer to the same entity, is −13.29. From this starting point, we add a match weight of 20.92 when we find an exact match of the CompanyName "Bespoke Crew." This represents the degree to which it's more likely to find exact equivalence on CompanyName within the match population than within the notmatch population.

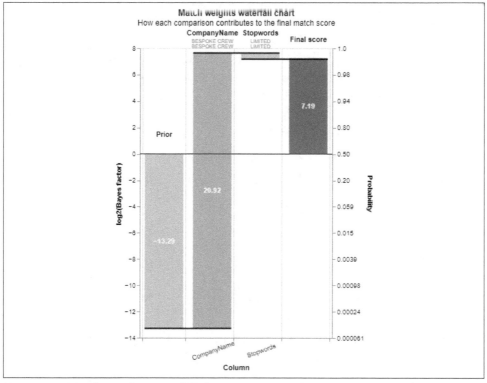

Figure 6-6. Match weights waterfall chart

However, we also need to subtract 0.45 due to the exact match on "Limited," as an exact equivalent on stopwords is more likely to occur on notmatches as opposed to matches. This gives us a final match weight of 7.19, which translates into a probability of almost 1.0.

Measuring Performance

After standardizing, the MCA data has 96 organizations.

At a 0.05 match threshold, our results are shown in Table 6-2.

Table 6-2. MCA match results—low threshold

Match threshold = 0.05	Number of matches	Unique entities matched
Name and postcode match	47	45
Name match only	37	31
Postcode match only	116	27
Total matches	**200**	**85 (deduped)**
Unmatched		11 (of which 2 dissolved)
Total organizations		**96**

If we assume the deduped unique matches are true positive matches, 9 of the 11 unmatched entities are false negatives, and the 2 dissolved entities are true negatives, then we can evaluate our performance as:

$$True\,positive\,matches\,(TP) = 85$$

$$False\,positive\,matches\,(FP) = 200 - 85 = 115$$

$$False\,negative\,matches\,(FN) = 11 - 2 = 9$$

$$True\,negatives = 2$$

$$Precision = \frac{TP}{(TP+FP)} = \frac{85}{(85+115)} \approx 42\,\%$$

$$Recall = \frac{TP}{(TP+FN)} = \frac{85}{(85+9)} \approx 90\,\%$$

$$Accuracy = \frac{(TP+TN)}{(TP+TN+FP+FN)} = \frac{(85+2)}{(85+2+115+9)} \approx 41\,\%$$

Recalculating our predictions at a threshold of 0.9 removes postcode-only matches, giving us the results shown in Table 6-3.

Table 6-3. MCA match result—high threshold

Match threshold = 0.9	Number of matches	Unique entities matched
Name and postcode match	47	45
Name match only	37	31
Postcode match only	3	1
Total matches	**87**	**73 (deduped)**
Unmatched		23 (of which 2 dissolved)
Total organizations		**96**

$$True\ positive\ matches\ (TP) = 73$$

$$False\ positive\ matches\ (FP) = 87 - 73 = 14$$

$$False\ negative\ matches\ (FN) = 23 - 2 = 21$$

$$True\ negatives = 2$$

$$Precision = \frac{TP}{(TP + FP)} = \frac{73}{(73 + 14)} \approx 84\%$$

$$Recall = \frac{TP}{(TP + FN)} = \frac{73}{(73 + 21)} \approx 78\%$$

$$Accuracy = \frac{(TP + TN)}{(TP + TN + FP + FN)} = \frac{(73 + 2)}{(73 + 2 + 14 + 21)} \approx 69\%$$

Therefore, as expected, we see that a higher match threshold increases our precision from 42% to 86%, but at the cost of missing nearly twice as many potential matches (up from 9 to 21 false negatives).

Tuning an entity resolution solution requires a degree of trial and error, adjusting blocking rules, similarity thresholds, and overall match thresholds to find the optimum balance. This will depend heavily on the characteristics of your data and your risk appetite for failing to identify potential matches.

Matching New Entities

As we have seen, model training is not a quick process. What if we have a new entity, say a new entry onto the MCA list, that we'd like to resolve against the Companies House data? Splink provides the option to match new records against previously matched datasets without retraining. We can also use this feature to find all potential matches, without the constraint of blocking rules or match thresholds, to help us understand why those candidates weren't identified. For example, if we take the last entity in our unmatched population:

```
record = {
    'unique_id': 1,
    'Postcode': "BH15 4QE",
    'CompanyName':"VANTAGE YACHT RECRUITMENT",
    'Stopwords':""
}

df_new = linker.find_matches_to_new_records([record],
    match_weight_threshold=0).as_pandas_dataframe()
df_new.sort_values("match_weight", ascending=False)
```

This results in a full list of candidate matches, the first four of which, with the highest match probabilities, are listed in Figure 6-7.

match_weight	match_probability	unique_id_l	unique_id_r	CompanyName_l	CompanyName_r	gamma_CompanyName	bf_CompanyName	Postcode_l	Postcode_r
8.645028	0.997508	93	1	VANTAGE YACHT RECRUITMENT	VANTAGE YACHT RECRUITMENT	3	4.002849e+06	BH15 4QE	BH15 4QE
1.275890	0.707729	5014788	1	VANTAGE YACHTING	VANTAGE YACHT RECRUITMENT	2	2.421239e+04	BH19 2PQ	BH15 4QE
1.275890	0.707729	5014331	1	VANTAGE AUTO RECRUITMENT	VANTAGE YACHT RECRUITMENT	2	2.421239e+04	DA1 1RZ	BH15 4QE
1.275890	0.707729	5014477	1	VANTAGE HEALTHCARE RECRUITMENT	VANTAGE YACHT RECRUITMENT	2	2.421239e+04	MK14 6GD	BH15 4QE

Figure 6-7. New potential matches

The first entry in the table is the original record in the MCA dataset. The next three records, as candidates matches from the Companies House data, don't have exact postcodes or name matches and so would have been excluded by our blocking rules. However, the second record does have a somewhat similar name and a close match on postcode and so looks like a good potential candidate.

Summary

In this chapter, we used a combination of name and address matching to resolve company entities across two datasets. We separated stopwords from our organization names and employed a regular expression to extract postcodes for comparison.

We used exact equivalence blocking rules and then calculated our match probabilities based on name similarity above a threshold. We evaluated our results by examining the trade-off between setting a low match threshold that produced a relatively large number of false positives and using a high threshold with the consequence that we missed some potentially promising match candidates.

This chapter has also illustrated that, even employing blocking techniques, entity resolution at scale can become a time-consuming and compute-intensive task. In subsequent chapters we will examine how to leverage cloud computing infrastructure to distribute our matching workload across a number of machines in parallel.

CHAPTER 7

Clustering

So far, we have considered the resolution of entities between two independent data sources: a smaller primary dataset that defines a target population to be matched and a much larger secondary dataset. We have also assumed that the entities in the primary dataset are present only once and there are no duplicates. Therefore, we have not sought to compare the entities in the primary dataset with each other.

For example, in Chapter 5, we resolved UK MPs, as listed in Wikipedia, against PSCs of UK companies according to Companies House. We assumed that each MP would be present only once in the Wikipedia list but that they could have significant control over more than one company, i.e., a single Wikipedia entity could match against multiple PSC entities. For instance, the MP named in Wikipedia as Geoffrey Clifton-Brown is likely to be the same individual as the person with the same name listed as having significant control over the company with reference number 09199367. The same applies to the companies with references 02303726 and 13420433.

We can represent these entity relationships as a simple network with the similarly named individuals represented as *nodes* and the three pairwise comparisons between them represented as *edges*, as shown in Figure 7-1.

Note that we didn't evaluate the pairwise equivalence of the three named individuals in the PSC data with each other—we were seeking only to identify links to the primary Wikipedia entity. But in the process we have, by association, concluded that all three PSC entries are likely to refer to the same single real-world individual.

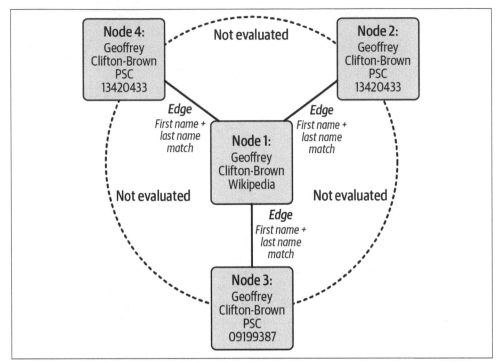

Figure 7-1. Simple person match cluster

In practice we are often faced with multiple data sources to resolve, as well as potential duplication within a single source. To produce a resolved view of an entity, we need to gather together all the pair-matched records, grouping them under a single uniquely identifiable reference.

This process of assembling a collection of examples is called *clustering*. The clustering process doesn't attempt to determine which example (if any) is correct but simply to identify the collection as a discrete bounded set whose members all have similar characteristics.

In this chapter, we will examine how to employ basic clustering techniques to group entities together based on pairwise comparisons. We will reuse the PSC dataset we acquired in Chapter 5, but first, let's shrink the problem to a small scale so that we can understand the steps we need to take.

Simple Exact Match Clustering

First, let's consider a simple dataset of first names, last names, and year of birth, as shown in Table 7-1. This table contains an exact duplicate (IDs 0 and 1) along with several other similar records.

Table 7-1. Simple clustering example dataset

ID	First name	Last name	Year of birth
0	Michael	Shearer	1970
1	Michael	Shearer	1970
2	Mike	Shearer	1970
3	Michael	Shearer	1971
4	Michelle	Shearer	1971
5	Mike	Sheare	1971

Does each ID represent a separate entity or do they refer to the same person?

Based on the limited information we have, we can, for example, group by exact equivalence of first name and last name but not year of birth.

```
table = [
    [0,'Michael','Shearer',1970],
    [1,'Michael','Shearer',1970],
    [2,'Mike','Shearer',1970],
    [3,'Michael','Shearer',1971],
    [4,'Michelle','Shearer',1971],
    [5,'Mike','Sheare',1971]]

clmns = ['ID','Firstname','Lastname','Year']
df_ms = pd.DataFrame(table, columns = clmns)

df_ms['cluster'] =
    df_ms.groupby(['Firstname','Lastname']).ngroup()
```

This gives us four clusters. The entities associated with IDs 0, 1, and 3 are grouped together in cluster 0 as they have the exact same name spellings, whereas IDs 2, 4, and 5 have a unique spelling variation and are therefore assigned their own individual cluster, as we can see in Figure 7-2.

	ID	Firstname	Lastname	Year	cluster
0	0	Michael	Shearer	1970	0
1	1	Michael	Shearer	1970	0
2	2	Mike	Shearer	1970	3
3	3	Michael	Shearer	1971	0
4	4	Michelle	Shearer	1971	1
5	5	Mike	Sheare	1971	2

Figure 7-2. Simple exact match cluster table

Approximate Match Clustering

Now let's consider what happens to our cluster groupings if we include approximate name matching, as introduced in Chapter 3. We can no longer use a simple `groupby` function to calculate our clusters, so we need to work through the comparison steps ourselves. This is a helpful exercise to illustrate the combined challenge that comes with comparing records within, and across, large datasets.

Our first step is to generate a table with all the potential combinations of record comparisons. We want to compare the record ID 0 with each of the other records and then the record ID 1 with the remainder, but without duplicating the comparison with ID 0 again (directionality isn't important in pairwise comparisons). In total we have 15 comparisons: 5 for ID 0 against its peers, 4 for ID 1, and so on.

From our simple base table we can use the itertools package we introduced in Chapter 3 to generate a DataFrame with composite columns A and B, each containing a list of the attributes to be compared drawn from our simple table:

```
import itertools

df_combs = pd.DataFrame(list(itertools.combinations(table,2)),
    columns=['A','B'])
```

Figure 7-3 shows the first few rows of the DataFrame.

	A	B
0	[0, Michael, Shearer, 1970]	[1, Michael, Shearer, 1970]
1	[0, Michael, Shearer, 1970]	[2, Mike, Shearer, 1970]
2	[0, Michael, Shearer, 1970]	[3, Michael, Shearer, 1971]

Figure 7-3. Sample rows of composite match combinations

Next, we need to create the multilevel index columns to hold the individual attribute values under the A and B headings:

```
clmnsA = pd.MultiIndex.from_arrays([['A']*len(clmns), clmns])
clmnsB = pd.MultiIndex.from_arrays([['B']*len(clmns), clmns])
```

Now we can split out the attributes and recombine the resulting columns, with their associated index labels, back to a single DataFrame:

```
df_edges = pd.concat(
    [pd.DataFrame(df_combs['A'].values.tolist(),columns = clmnsA),
     pd.DataFrame(df_combs['B'].values.tolist(),columns = clmnsB)],
    axis=1)
```

The first few expanded rows are shown in Figure 7-4.

		A				B			
	ID	Firstname	Lastname	Year	ID	Firstname	Lastname	Year
0	0	Michael	Shearer	1970	1	Michael	Shearer	1970
1	0	Michael	Shearer	1970	2	Mike	Shearer	1970
2	0	Michael	Shearer	1970	3	Michael	Shearer	1971

Figure 7-4. Sample rows of approximate match combinations

Now that we have our attributes prepared for pairwise evaluation, we can use the Jaro-Winkler similarity function introduced in Chapter 3 to approximately compare the first names and last names between the A and B values. If both match, say with an equivalence score greater than 0.9, then we declare an overall match:

```
import jellyfish as jf

def is_match(row):
    firstname_match = jf.jaro_winkler_similarity(row['A']
        ['Firstname'],row['B']['Firstname']) > 0.9
    lastname_match = jf.jaro_winkler_similarity(row['A']
        ['Lastname'], row['B']['Lastname']) > 0.9
    return firstname_match and lastname_match

df_edges['Match'] = df_edges.apply(is_match, axis=1)

df_edges
```

The resulting matches are listed in Figure 7-5. We can see that record ID 0 matches exactly with ID 1 and ID 3 on rows 0 and 2, respectively. A match is also declared on row 3 between ID 0 and ID 4 as there is sufficient similarity between "Michael" and "Michelle." Note that rows 6, 7, and 12 also record direct matches between the remaining combinations of IDs 1, 3, and 4 independent of ID 0.

ID 2 also matches to ID 5 on row 11 with "Shearer" and "Sheare" being sufficiently similar.

	A				B				Match
	ID	Firstname	Lastname	Year	ID	Firstname	Lastname	Year	
0	0	Michael	Shearer	1970	1	Michael	Shearer	1970	True
1	0	Michael	Shearer	1970	2	Mike	Shearer	1970	False
2	0	Michael	Shearer	1970	3	Michael	Shearer	1971	True
3	0	Michael	Shearer	1970	4	Michelle	Shearer	1971	True
4	0	Michael	Shearer	1970	5	Mike	Sheare	1971	False
5	1	Michael	Shearer	1970	2	Mike	Shearer	1970	False
6	1	Michael	Shearer	1970	3	Michael	Shearer	1971	True
7	1	Michael	Shearer	1970	4	Michelle	Shearer	1971	True
8	1	Michael	Shearer	1970	5	Mike	Sheare	1971	False
9	2	Mike	Shearer	1970	3	Michael	Shearer	1971	False
10	2	Mike	Shearer	1970	4	Michelle	Shearer	1971	False
11	2	Mike	Shearer	1970	5	Mike	Sheare	1971	True
12	3	Michael	Shearer	1971	4	Michelle	Shearer	1971	True
13	3	Michael	Shearer	1971	5	Mike	Sheare	1971	False
14	4	Michelle	Shearer	1971	5	Mike	Sheare	1971	False

Figure 7-5. Approximate match table

From these results we can manually identify two clusters, the first comprising IDs 0, 1, 3, and 4 and the second IDs 2 and 5.

NetworkX

NetworkX is an open source Python package for the creation, manipulation, and study of the structure, dynamics, and functions of complex networks.

We can use NetworkX to calculate our clusters. For this simple example, we map the entity IDs as the nodes of a network graph and the binary pairwise comparisons as the edges. From this graph object, we can use the connected components algorithm to derive the resulting clusters:

```
import networkx as nx
G = nx.from_pandas_edgelist(df_edges[df_edges['Match']],
    source=('A','ID'), target=('B','ID'))
list(nx.connected_components(G))

[{0, 1, 3, 4}, {2, 5}]
```

However, we are now faced with a problem. We have allowed nonexact matches to cluster as a single entity. What attribute values should we now use to describe that resolved entity? For the first cluster, comprising IDs 0, 1, 3, and 4, should the first name be "Michael" or "Michelle"? IDs 0, 1, and 3 have the first name as "Michael" but ID 4 has it listed as "Michelle." Is the correct year of birth 1970 or 1971?

For the second cluster, we face the same year of birth dilemma and the question of whether we should use "Sheare" or "Shearer"—it's not clear. This challenge, of selecting the most representative values, sometimes known as *canonicalization*, is a field of active study but beyond the scope of this book.

Even with this simple example we can see a number of challenges and trade-offs we need to consider when clustering entities together. First, the number of pairwise comparisons grows very rapidly with number of records to be clustered. For a table of n rows there are n × (n–1)/2 combinations. If approximate matches are included, the resulting computational burden is significant and may be time-consuming to compute. Second, and most challenging, is how to settle on a single set of attributes to define a cluster when individual entities within the cluster have differing attribute values.

Now that we have introduced some of the challenges associated with clustering, let's return to the PSC dataset to consider a larger-scale example.

Sample Problem

Returning to our example from Chapter 5, let's imagine we wish to examine the concentration of control over UK companies, identifying individuals with influence over several companies. To do this, we need to cluster all the matching individual owner entities in the PSC dataset. Further, knowing the variable data quality of PSC entries, let's consider that we want to incorporate approximate matches in our calculations.

With approximately 11.5 million entries in our PSC dataset, the total number of comparisons we need to make is over 66 trillion. We have our work cut out here!

Data Acquisition

Let's start by picking up the raw data we downloaded in Chapter 5. We'll use a wider range of attributes for matching in this chapter:

```
df_psc = pd.read_csv('psc_raw.csv',dtype=
    {'data.name_elements.surname':'string',
    'data.name_elements.forename':'string',
    'data.name_elements.middle_name':'string',
    'data.name_elements.title':'string',
    'data.nationality':'string'})
```

Data Standardization

Now that we have our raw data, our next step is to standardize and, for simplicity, rename the attributes. We also drop any records where the year or month of birth is missing because we'll use these as blocking values to help reduce the number of comparisons we need to make:

```
df_psc = df_psc.dropna(subset
    ['data.date_of_birth.year','data.date_of_birth.month'])
df_psc['Year'] = df_psc['data.date_of_birth.year'].astype('int64')
df_psc['Month'] =
    df_psc['data.date_of_birth.month'].astype('int64')

df_psc = df_psc.rename(columns=
    {"data.name_elements.surname" : "Lastname",
    "data.name_elements.forename" : "Firstname",
    "data.name_elements.middle_name" : "Middlename",
    "data.name_elements.title" : "Title",
    "data.nationality" : "Nationality"})

df_psc = df_psc[['Lastname','Middlename','Firstname',
    'company_number','Year','Month','Title','Nationality']]
df_psc['unique_id'] = df_psc.index
```

Record Blocking and Attribute Comparison

As before, we use the Splink framework to perform the comparisons, with exact equivalence on year, month, and last name as prediction blocking rules, i.e., we only compare records against each other if there are exact matches between the year, month, and last name fields. Clearly, this is a trade-off as we will potentially miss some matches with last name inconsistencies or spelling mistakes, for example.

Note that for this single source example we set the link_type to dedupe_only instead of link_only. Splink supports dedupe_only, link_only, and link_and_dedupe.

We also specify a convergence tolerance for the EM algorithm and set a maximum number of iterations to run (even if convergence has not been reached):

```
from splink.duckdb.linker import DuckDBLinker
from splink.duckdb import comparison_library as cl

settings = {
    "link_type": "dedupe_only",
    "blocking_rules_to_generate_predictions":
        [ "l.Year = r.Year and l.Month = r.Month and
            l.Lastname = r.Lastname" ],
    "comparisons":
        [ cl.jaro_winkler_at_thresholds("Firstname", [0.9]),
          cl.jaro_winkler_at_thresholds("Middlename", [0.9]),
          cl.exact_match("Lastname"),
          cl.exact_match("Title"),
          cl.exact_match("Nationality"),
          cl.exact_match("Month"),
          cl.exact_match("Year", term_frequency_adjustments=True), ],
    "retain_matching_columns": True,
    "retain_intermediate_calculation_columns": True,
    "max_iterations": 10,
    "em_convergence": 0.01,
    "additional_columns_to_retain": ["company_number"],
    }
linker = DuckDBLinker(df_psc, settings)
```

Data Analysis

As before, it's useful to have a look at the data distribution of our comparison attributes:

```
linker.profile_columns(["Firstname","Middlename","Lastname",
    "Title","Nationality","Month","Year"], top_n=10, bottom_n=5)
```

As we can see in Figure 7-6, we have the expected distribution of first, middle, and last names. In Figure 7-7, we can also see that the distribution of title and nationality is skewed toward a small number of common values. Figure 7-8 shows month of birth is fairly evenly distributed across the year, whereas year of birth is somewhat skewed toward the 1980s.

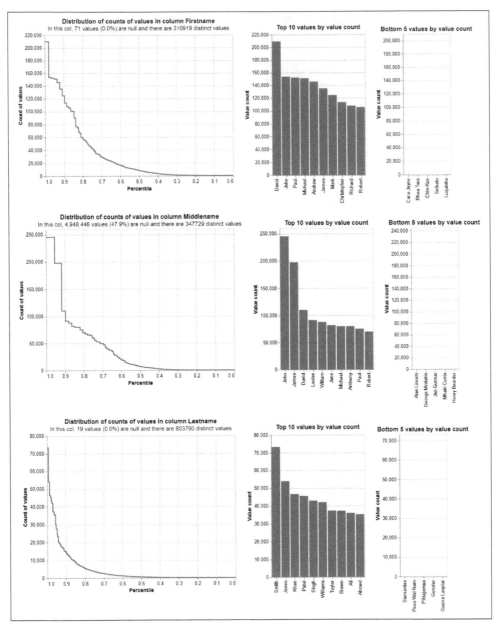

Figure 7-6. First name, middle name, and last name distribution

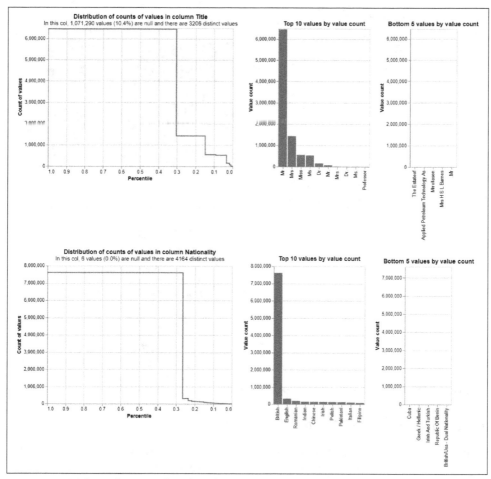

Figure 7-7. Title and nationality distribution

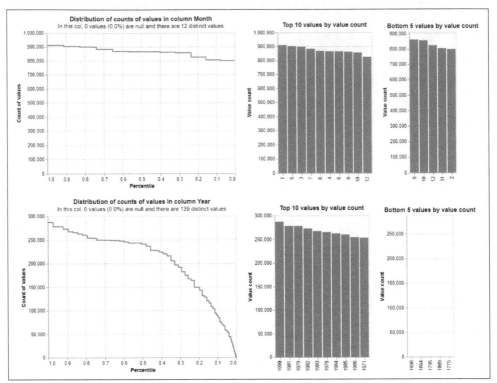

Figure 7-8. Year and month of birth distribution

Expectation-Maximization Blocking Rules

Given the very high number of potential combinations, we need to specify the blocking rules for the EM algorithm as tightly as we can to allow the process to complete in a reasonable timeframe.

We can test the volume of comparisons that a given blocking rule will generate using the `count_num_comparisons_from_blocking` function; for example:

```
linker.count_num_comparisons_from_blocking_rule(
    "l.Lastname = r.Lastname and
    l.Month = r.Month and
    l.Title = r.Title and
    l.Nationality = r.Nationality")
```

Remember that every attribute comparison level must pass the blocking rules (i.e., not be blocked) in at least one of the estimate parameter steps so that *m* and *u* values can be generated for that attribute.

The count of comparisons that would be generated for several combinations of attribute blocking rules is given in Table 7-2.

Table 7-2. Blocking rule comparison count

Pair	Attribute combination blocking rule	Count of comparisons
1	l.Lastname = r.Lastname and l.Month = r.Month and l.Title = r.Title and l.Nationality = r.Nationality	777.4M
	l.Firstname = r.Firstname and l.Year = r.Year and l.Middlename = r.Middlename	69.7M
2	l.Lastname = r.Lastname and l.Middlename = r.Middlename	119.9M
	l.Firstname = r.Firstname and l.Month = r.Month and l.Year = r.Year and l.Title = r.Title and l.Nationality = r.Nationality	281M

We can see that the first pair of blocking rules requires evaluation of a large number of comparisons, whereas the second pair allows estimation of parameters for all the attributes but with a smaller overall comparison count.

First name, middle name, and last name equivalences are the most discriminating in reducing the comparison volumes, followed by year of birth and to a lesser extent month of birth. Nationality and title are not particularly helpful due to limited cardinality of their values, as we saw in Figure 7-6.

We can employ these blocking rules as:

```
linker.estimate_parameters_using_expectation_maximisation(
    "l.Lastname = r.Lastname and l.Middlename = r.Middlename",
        fix_u_probabilities=False)

linker.estimate_parameters_using_expectation_maximisation(
    "l.Firstname = r.Firstname and l.Month = r.Month and
    l.Year = r.Year and l.Title = r.Title and
    l.Nationality = r.Nationality",
        fix_u_probabilities=False)
```

Computation Time

Even with these more optimized blocking rules, the execution of the expectation-maximization algorithm on a large dataset may take some time, especially if you're running on a modest machine.

Alternatively, if you want to skip the training step you can simply load the pretrained model using:

```
linker.load_settings("Chapter7_Splink_Settings.json")
```

Match Classification and Clustering

Once the EM step (see Chapter 4) is completed, we have a trained model to assess the similarity between the record pairs in our single dataset. Remember that these pairs are selected using the prediction blocking rules (in this case, exact last name, year, and month of birth). The threshold for predicting a match is set at 0.9:

```
df_predict = linker.predict(threshold_match_probability=0.9)
```

Following pairwise prediction, Splink offers a clustering function to group entity pairs together when the match probability to a shared entity exceeds a specified threshold. Note that the clustering threshold is applied to the full set of pairwise combinations, not the subset that exceeds the 0.9 prediction threshold; i.e., records that fell below the equivalence threshold in all their comparisons, and thus were not paired at all, will still be present in the output, assigned to their own cluster:

```
clusters = linker.cluster_pairwise_predictions_at_threshold(
    df_predict, threshold_match_probability=0.9)
df_clusters = clusters.as_pandas_dataframe()

df_clusters.head(n=5)
```

The resulting dataset of records, labeled with their parent cluster, can easily be converted to a DataFrame, the first few rows of which (sanitized to remove names and year and month of birth) are shown in Figure 7-9.

	cluster_id	Lastname	Middlename	Firstname	company_number	Year	Month	Title	Nationality	unique_id	tf_Year
0	3905351				11210696			Mrs	British	5020528	0.025653
1	5019648				SC589021			Mrs	British	5019648	0.025653
2	5019715				11210203			Mr	British	5019715	0.014424
3	377809				NI642840			Mr	British	5019804	0.018575
4	2861408				SC588975			Mr	British	5019268	0.025157

Figure 7-9. Sample rows

We can then group these rows by `cluster_id`, retaining all the different attribute values from each source record in a list under the associated column. In our case, no variation is expected on last name, month, or year of birth as we generated our predictions using exact equivalence of these attributes as our blocking rules. This gives us approximately 6.8 million unique clusters:

```
df_cgroup =
    df_clusters.groupby(['cluster_id'], sort=False)
        [['company_number','Firstname','Title','Nationality','Lastname']]
            .agg(lambda x: list(set(x)))
                .reset_index()
```

To illustrate the attribute variation we see within a cluster, we can select a subset of clusters where we have differing first names, titles, and nationalities. For ease of manual examination, we limit ourselves to clusters compromising exactly six records:

```
df_cselect = df_cgroup[
    (df_cgroup['Firstname'].apply(len) > 1) &
    (df_cgroup['Title'].apply(len) > 1) &
    (df_cgroup['Nationality'].apply(len) > 1) &
    (df_cgroup['company_number'].apply(len) == 6)]

df_cselect.head(n=5)
```

In the resulting sanitized table, shown in Figure 7-10, we can see a selection of these clusters in tabular form.

cluster_id	company_number	Firstname	Title	Nationality	Lastname
888855	[SC636515, SC763002, SC547161, SC782674, SC637...		[Mr, nan]	[British, Scottish]	
2914432	[12442210, 14418516, 13437477, 10708630, 13410...		[Mr, nan]	[British, Pakistani]	
3423125	[10160770, SC585125, 11601885, 11210167, SC773...		[Mr, nan]	[Pakistani, British]	
2338441	[OE019853, 09498780, OE016371, 04559738, 07672...		[Mr, nan]	[British, British,]	
2616813	[11597840, 14157360, 14952153, 14455516, 10668...		[Mr, nan]	[British, Italian, Indian]	

Figure 7-10. Sample rows showing attribution variation in clusters of size six

Cluster Visualization

Now that we have our PSCs clustered together, we can perform a count of the number of companies each entity controls and then plot the distribution of these values in a histogram:

```
import matplotlib.pyplot as plt
import numpy as np

mybins =[1,2,10,100,1000,10000]
fig, ax = plt.subplots()
counts, bins, patches = ax.hist(df_cgroup['unique_id'].apply(len),
    bins=mybins )
bin_centers = 0.5 * np.diff(bins) + bins[:-1]

for label, x in zip(['1','2-10','10-100','100-1000','1000+'],
    bin_centers):
    ax.annotate(label, xy=(x, 0), xycoords=('data', 'axes fraction'),
                xytext=(0,-10), textcoords='offset points', va='top',
                ha='right')
ax.tick_params(labelbottom=False)
ax.xaxis.set_label_coords(0,-0.1)
ax.xaxis.set_tick_params(which='minor', bottom=False)

ax.set_xlabel('Number of controlled companies')
ax.set_ylabel('Count')
```

```
ax.set_title('Distribution of significant company control')
ax.set_yscale('log')
ax.set_xscale('log')

fig.tight_layout()
plt.show()
```

Figure 7-11 shows the resulting plot, which allows us to begin to answer our sample question—how concentrated is the control of UK companies? We can see that the majority of individuals control only a single company, with a smaller, but still very significant, number having influence over between 2 and 10 firms. After that, the count falls dramatically until our data suggests that we have a handful of individuals with influence over more than 1,000 companies.

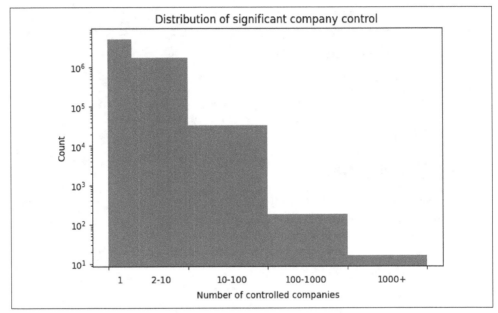

Figure 7-11. Histogram distribution of significant company control

If, like me, you think the significant control of over 1,000 companies sounds a little unlikely, then it's time we examine our clustering results in a little more detail to see what may be going on. To get a feel for the issues, let's look at the subset of clusters formed from exactly six records.

Cluster Analysis

Splink provides us with a cluster studio dashboard, which we can interact with to explore the clusters we have generated to understand how they have been formed.

The dashboard is persisted as an HTML page that we can display within the Jupyter environment as a Python inline frame (IFrame):

```
linker.cluster_studio_dashboard(df_predict, clusters,
    "Chapter7_cluster_studio.html",
    cluster_ids = df_cselect['cluster_id'].to_list(), overwrite=True)

from IPython.display import IFrame
IFrame( src="Chapter7_cluster_studio.html", width="100%",
    height=1200)
```

Figure 7-12 shows an example of the studio dashboard.

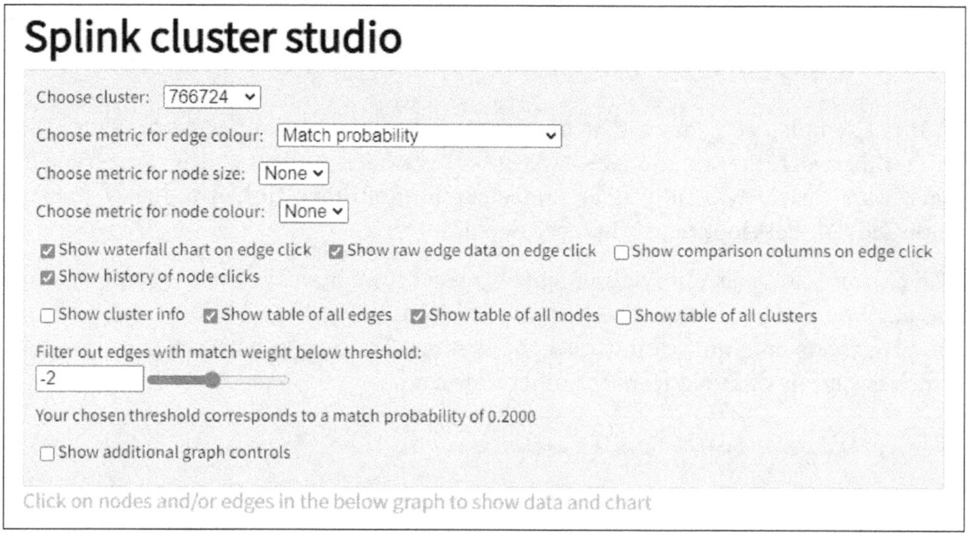

Figure 7-12. Splink cluster studio dashboard

Let's consider an example cluster, reference: 766724.[1] Remember that all the nodes in this cluster share the exact matches on the same last name, month, and year of birth due to the blocking rules.

The cluster studio provides a graph view of each cluster with the nodes labeled with their assigned unique identifier and linked together with edges associated with each of the pairwise comparisons that exceeded the set threshold. This is shown in Figure 7-13.

---

1 Note: If you are following along with your own notebook and PSC dataset, your cluster references may vary.

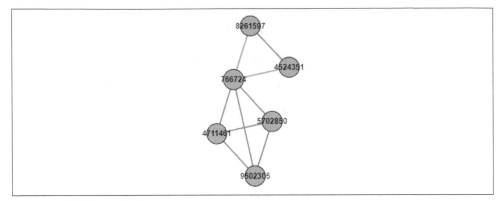

Figure 7-13. Example cluster

In this example, we can see that not all of the nodes are connected to each other. In fact, between the 6 nodes we have only 9 connected edges out of a possible 15. There are clearly two fully interconnected mini-clusters, linked together through node 766724. Let's look at this in more detail.

The cluster studio also provides a tabular view of the nodes so that we can examine the attributes in more detail, as shown sanitized in Figure 7-14. We have sanitized the Firstname column—in this case, the first and third rows have the same spelling, which is slightly different from the other four rows.

cluster_id	Lastname	Middlename	Firstname	company_number	Year	Month	Title	Nationality	unique_id	tf_Year
766,724				11138256			Mr	British	4,524,351	0.024
766,724				09750945				British	766,724	0.024
766,724				13647634			Mr	British	8,261,597	0.024
766,724				11261953			Mr	English	4,711,461	0.024
766,724				14495151			Mr	English	9,502,305	0.024
766,724				11928604			Mr	English	5,702,850	0.024

Figure 7-14. Example cluster nodes

The top mini-cluster of nodes 8261597, 4524351, and 766724 all have the same Nationality and are also missing a Middlename. The second mini-cluster of nodes 766724, 5702850, 4711461, and 9502305 all have exactly matching Firstname values.

The sanitized tabular edge view, shown in Figure 7-15, gives us the match weights and associated probabilities for these pairwise comparisons.

match_weight	match_probability	unique_id_l	unique_id_r
14.146	1	4,711,461	5,702,850
14.146	1	4,711,461	9,502,305
14.146	1	5,702,850	9,502,305
3.261	0.906	766,724	8,261,597
3.261	0.906	766,724	4,524,351
8.844	0.998	766,724	5,702,850
8.844	0.998	766,724	4,711,461
8.844	0.998	766,724	9,502,305
8.536	0.997	4,524,351	8,261,597

Figure 7-15. Example cluster edges

If we increase our match threshold to filter out edges with a match weight threshold below 3.4, we break the two lowest scoring pairwise links. As seen in Figure 7-16, our second mini-cluster remains intact but our first mini-cluster has broken apart, with nodes 8261597 and 4524351 now separate due to their different first name spelling.

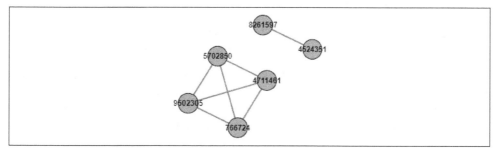

Figure 7-16. Example clusters—high match threshold

Further increasing the match weight threshold to 8.7 breaks our first mini-cluster completely as the lack of Middlename becomes a deciding negative factor. This is shown in Figure 7-17.

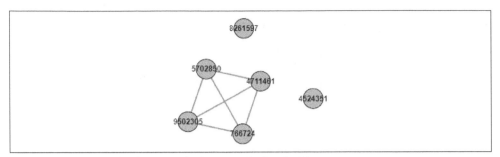

Figure 7-17. Example clusters—higher match threshold

Increasing the match weight to a very high threshold of 9.4 causes node 766724 to break apart due to its slightly different first name spelling, as shown in Figure 7-18.

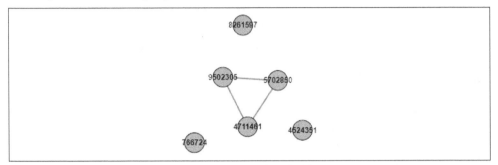

Figure 7-18. Example clusters—highest match threshold

As we can see, the size and density of our clusters is highly dependent upon the thresholds we set for grouping pairwise comparisons together.

The Companies House website gives us access to information on the address associated with these PSC records. Company numbers 8261597, 4711461, and 4524351 were all registered by an individual giving the same address, as were 5702850 and 9502305. This gives us more confidence that this cluster does indeed represent one individual.

A wider review suggests that our first pass at assessing the concentration of control over UK companies was perhaps too optimistic. Setting our match and clustering thresholds at 0.9 has erred toward overlinking, resulting in larger clusters with weaker associations. This may go some way to explain the rather dubious assessment of several individuals with significant control of more than 1,000 companies.

I hope that working through this sample problem has illustrated that entity resolution with messy real-world data is not an exact science. There is no single right answer, and judgment is needed to set the matching thresholds to the optimum values for the outcomes you are seeking to achieve.

Summary

In this chapter, we have seen how entity resolution within and across multiple datasets can produce a large number of pairwise comparisons. We learned how to select and evaluate blocking rules to reduce these combinations to a more practical volume to allow us to train and then run our matching algorithm in a reasonable timeframe.

Using approximate matching and probabilistic entity resolution, we were able to generate clusters from pairwise comparisons, allowing for variations in some of the attributes. However, we were left with the canonicalization challenge of how to decide which attribute values to use to describe our unified entity.

We also learned how to use graph visualizations to help us understand our clusters. We saw how cluster size and composition is strongly influenced by our choice of match threshold and that the risks of over- or underlinking need to be balanced in the context of a particular dataset and desired outcome.

CHAPTER 8

Scaling Up on Google Cloud

In this chapter, we will work through how to scale up our entity resolution process to enable us to match large datasets in reasonable timeframes. We will use a cluster of virtual machines running in parallel on Google Cloud Platform (GCP) to divide up the workload and reduce the time taken to resolve our entities.

We will walk through how to register a new account on the Cloud Platform and how to configure the storage and compute services we will need. Once our infrastructure is ready, we will rerun our company matching example from Chapter 6, splitting both model training and entity resolution steps across a managed cluster of compute resources.

Lastly, we will check that our performance is consistent and make sure we tidy up fully, deleting the cluster and returning the virtual machines we have borrowed to ensure we don't continue to run up any additional fees.

Google Cloud Platform

Google Cloud Platform (GCP) is an integrated set of compute, storage, data, and analytics products. End users, from individuals to large enterprises, can rent capacity on these platforms. Amazon and Microsoft offer similar environments.

The ability to temporarily hire computing facilities at an affordable rate, and without the large up-front cost of purchasing additional hardware, is ideal for development, testing, and educational purposes.

In production the scalable nature of these cloud platforms is ideal for "peaky" workloads, like batch entity resolution jobs, which periodically require a sizeable compute infrastructure for a short period of time before often sitting idle until the next scheduled job. Using a cloud provider you can set up your operations so that you pay only for the capacity you use, offering substantial savings against a poorly utilized standing IT estate.

Google Cloud Setup

To build our cloud infrastructure, we first need to register for an account on the GCP. To do this, visit *cloud.google.com* on your browser. From here, you can click Get Started to begin the registration process. You'll need to register with a Google email address or alternatively create a new account. This is shown in Figure 8-1.

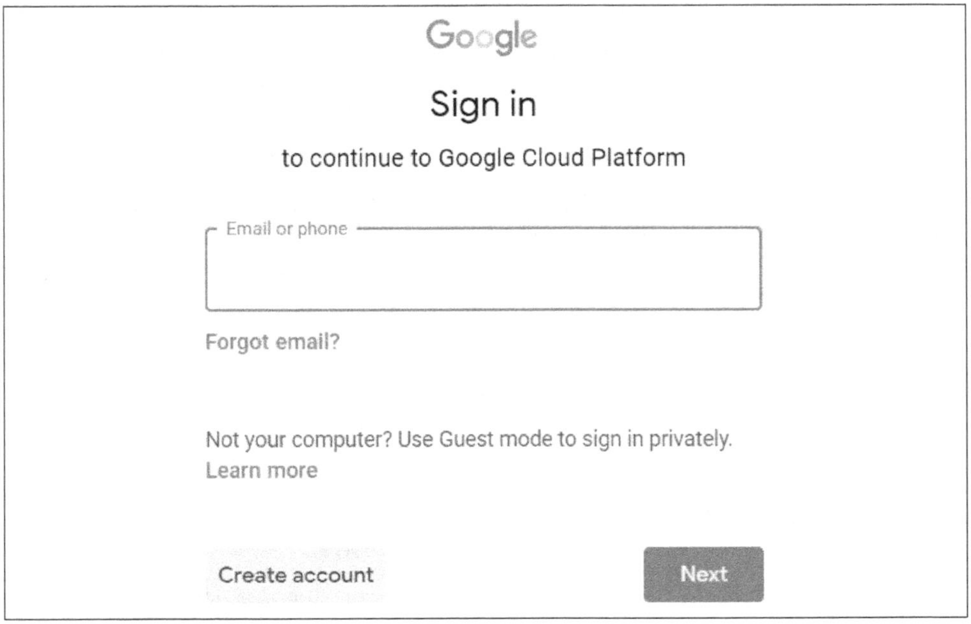

Figure 8-1. GCP sign in

You'll need to select your country, read and then accept the Google terms of service, and click Continue. See Figure 8-2.

Step 1 of 2 Account Information

SWITCH ACCOUNT

Country

United Kingdom ▼

What best describes your organization or needs?

Please select ▼

Terms of Service

☐ I have read and agree to the Google Cloud Platform Terms of
Service, Supplemental Free Trial Terms of Service, and the terms of
service of any applicable services and APIs.

Required to continue

Figure 8-2. Register for GCP, Account Information Step 1

On the next page, you will be asked to verify your address and payment information
before you can click Start My Free Trial.

Google Cloud Platform Fees

Please be warned that it's your responsibility to understand the
ongoing charges associated with using any of the products on the
Google Cloud Platform. From personal experience I can say it is
very easy to leave virtual machines running or overlook persistent
disks that you will still be charged for.

At the time of writing, Google Cloud is offering $300 credit for free
to spend over the first 90 days of your usage of the platform. They
are also stating that no autocharge will be applied after the free trial
ends, so if you use a credit or debit card, you won't be charged
unless you manually upgrade to a paid account.

*Of course, these terms are subject to change, so please read the terms
carefully when you sign up.*

Once you've signed up, you'll be taken to the Google Cloud console.

Setting Up Project Storage

Your first task is to create a project. On GCP, a project is a logical group of resources and data that you manage. For the purpose of this book, all our work will be grouped together in one project.

To begin, choose your preferred project name and Google will suggest a corresponding Project ID for you. You might wish to edit their suggestion to shorten or simplify it a little as you'll potentially be typing in this Project ID a fair number of times.

As an individual user, you don't need to specify an organization owner of your project, as illustrated in Figure 8-3.

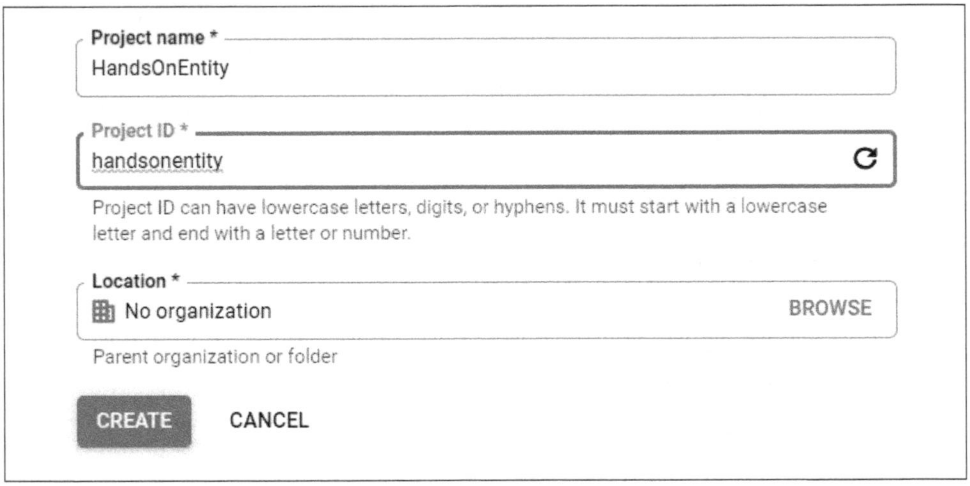

```
┌─ Project name * ──────────────────────────────────────────┐
│  HandsOnEntity                                            │
└────────────────────────────────────────────────────────────┘

┌─ Project ID * ────────────────────────────────────────────┐
│  handsonentity                                        ⟳   │
└────────────────────────────────────────────────────────────┘
Project ID can have lowercase letters, digits, or hyphens. It must start with a lowercase
letter and end with a letter or number.

┌─ Location * ──────────────────────────────────────────────┐
│  ▦ No organization                              BROWSE    │
└────────────────────────────────────────────────────────────┘
Parent organization or folder

┌──────────┐
│  CREATE  │    CANCEL
└──────────┘
```

Figure 8-3. "Create a Project" dialog box

Once you've created your project, you'll be taken to the project dashboard.

The first thing we need is somewhere to store our data on GCP. The standard data storage product is called Cloud Storage, and within that, specific data containers are called buckets. Buckets have a globally unique name and a geographic location where the bucket and its data contents are stored. A bucket can have the same name as your Project ID if you wish.

To create a bucket, you can click on the navigation menu home (three horizontal lines within a circle, top left of the screen) to select Cloud Storage and then Buckets from the drop-down navigation menu. Figure 8-4 shows the menu options.

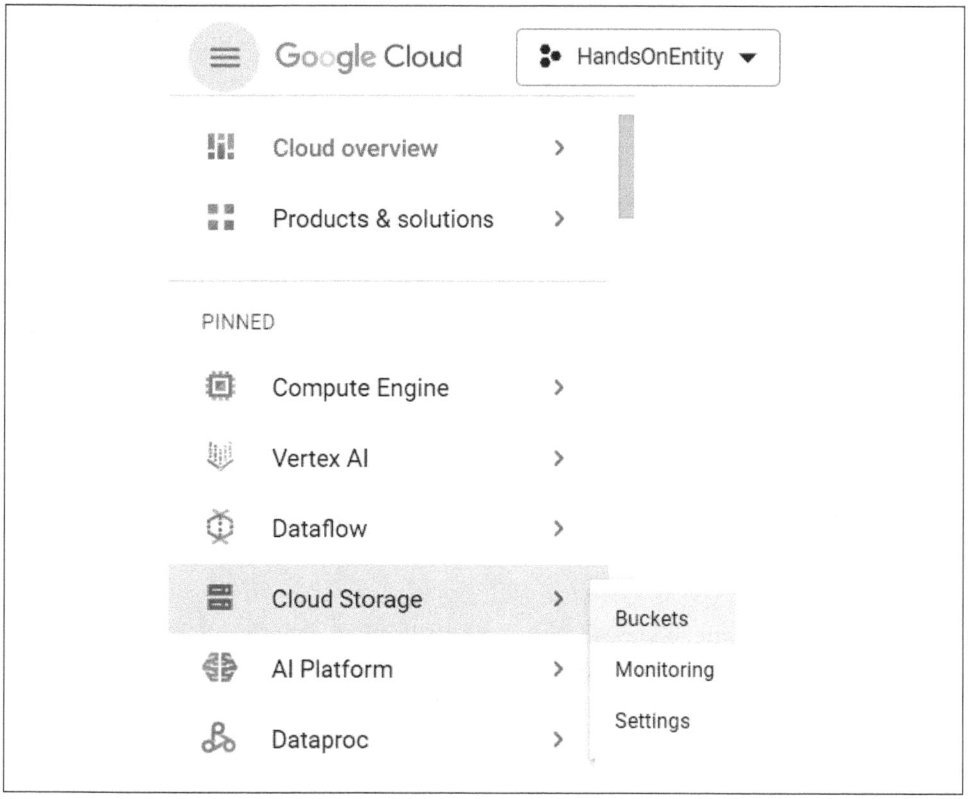

Figure 8-4. Navigation menu—Cloud Storage

From here, click Create Bucket from the menu at the top, select your preferred name, and then click Continue. See Figure 8-5.

Figure 8-5. Create bucket—naming

Next you need to select your preferred storage location, as illustrated in Figure 8-6. For the purposes of this project, you can accept the default or pick a different region if you prefer.

You can press Continue to view the remaining advanced configuration options or just jump straight to Create. Now that we have some storage space defined, our next step is to reserve some compute resources to run our entity resolution process.

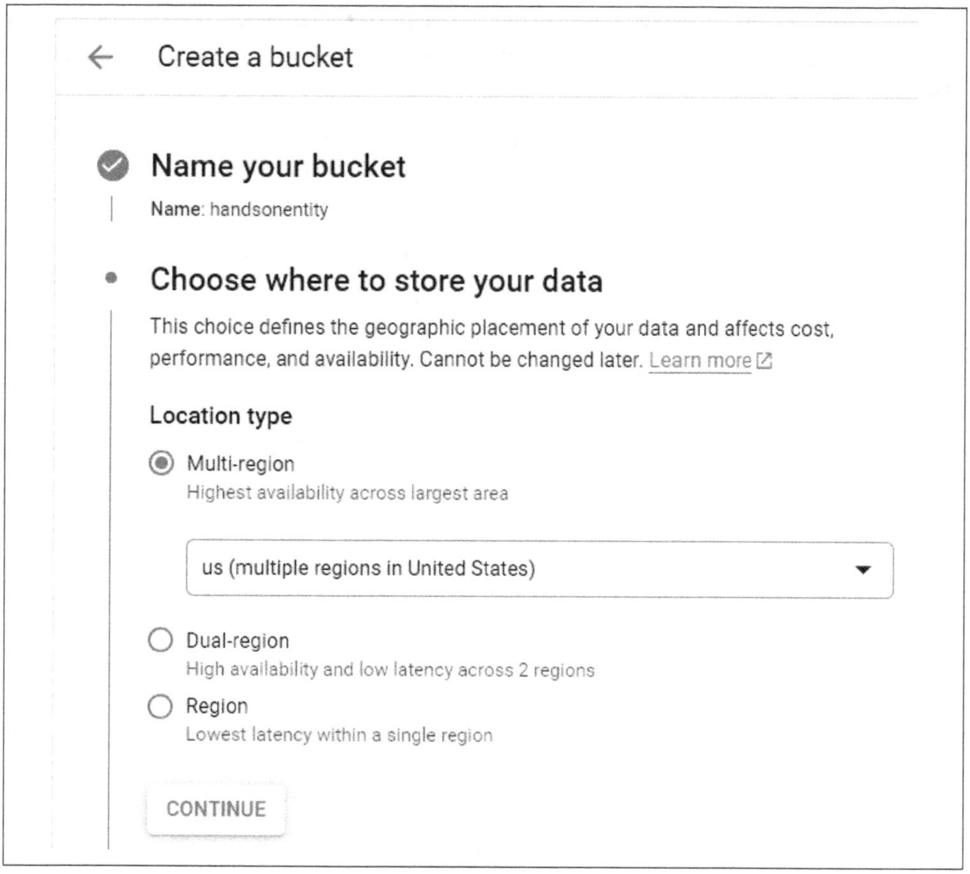

Figure 8-6. Create bucket—data storage location

Creating a Dataproc Cluster

As in previous chapters, we will be using the Splink framework to perform matching. To scale up our process to run across multiple machines, we need to switch from using DuckDB as our backend database to Spark.

Spark

Apache Spark is an analytics engine optimized for executing data processes on clusters of machines. It is open source and maintained by the Apache Software Foundation.

A convenient way to run Spark on the GCP is to use a *Dataproc cluster*, which takes care of creating a number of virtual machines and configuring them to execute a Spark job.

To create a cluster, we must first enable the Cloud Dataproc API. Return to the navigation menu and select Dataproc and then Clusters as per Figure 8-7.

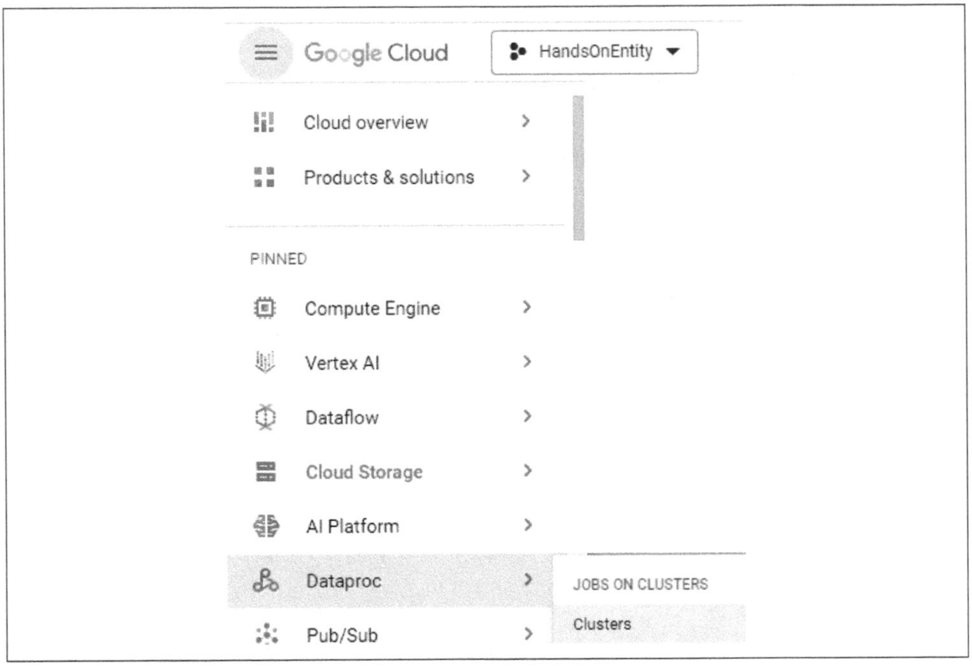

Figure 8-7. Navigation menu—Dataproc clusters

You'll then be presented with the API screen. Make sure you read and accept the terms and associated fees and then click Enable. See Figure 8-8.

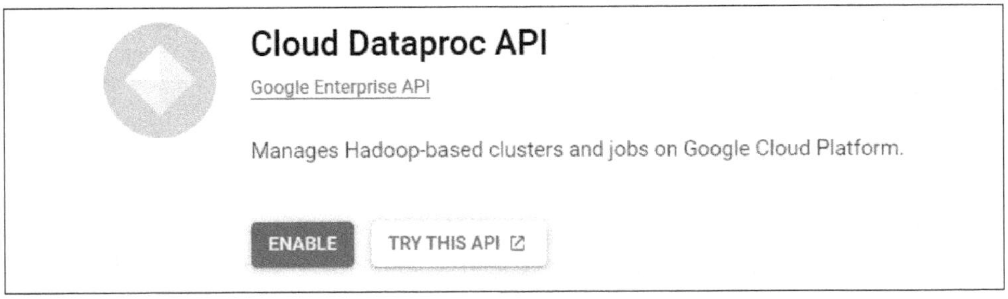

Figure 8-8. Enable the Cloud Dataproc API

Once the API is enabled, you can click on Create Cluster to configure your Dataproc instance. Dataproc clusters can be built directly on Compute Engine virtual machines or via GKE (Google Kubernetes Engine). For the purposes of this example, the distinction between the two isn't important, so I suggest you select Compute Engine as it is the simpler of the two.

You should then be presented with the screen in Figure 8-9.

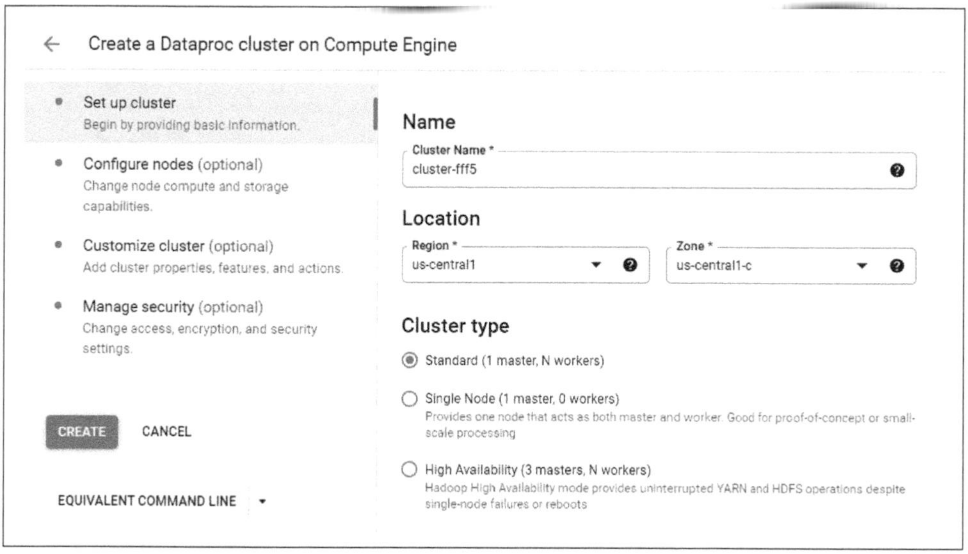

Figure 8-9. Create cluster on Compute Engine

Here you can name your cluster, select the location in which it resides, and choose the type of cluster. Next, scroll down to the Component section and select Component Gateway and Jupyter Notebook, as shown in Figure 8-10. This is important as it allows us to configure the cluster and use Jupyter to execute our entity resolution notebook.

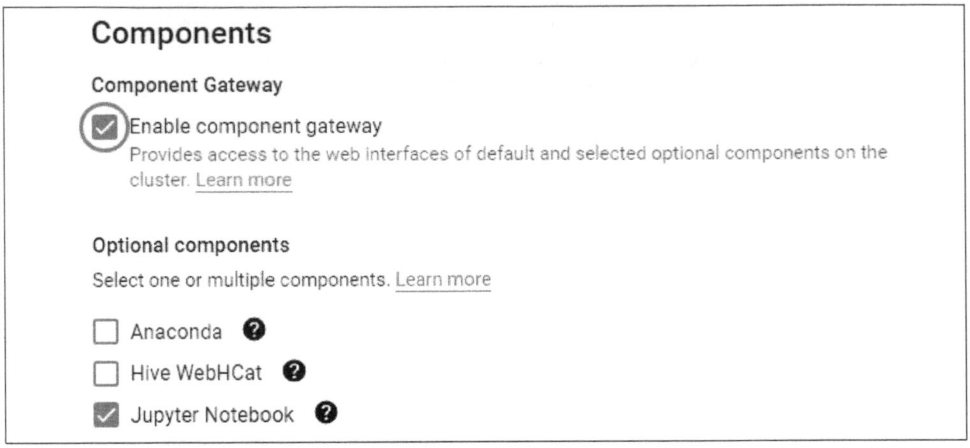

Figure 8-10. Dataproc components

Once you've configured the Components, you can accept the default settings for the rest of this page—see Figure 8-11—and then select the Configure Nodes option.

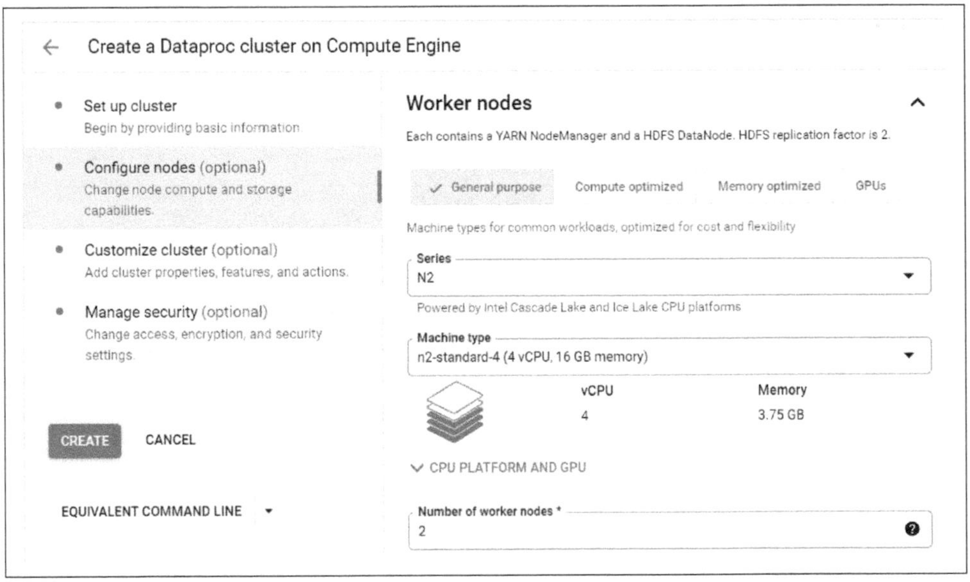

Figure 8-11. Configure worker nodes

The next step is to configure both the Manager and Worker nodes within our cluster. Again, you can accept the defaults, checking that the number of workers is set to 2 before moving on to Customize Cluster.

A final step, but an important one, is to consider scheduling deletion of the cluster to avoid any ongoing fees should you forget to remove your cluster manually when you're finished with it. I'd also recommend configuring the Cloud Storage staging bucket to use the bucket you created earlier; otherwise the Dataproc process will create a storage bucket for you that can easily get left behind in the clean-up operation. See Figure 8-12.

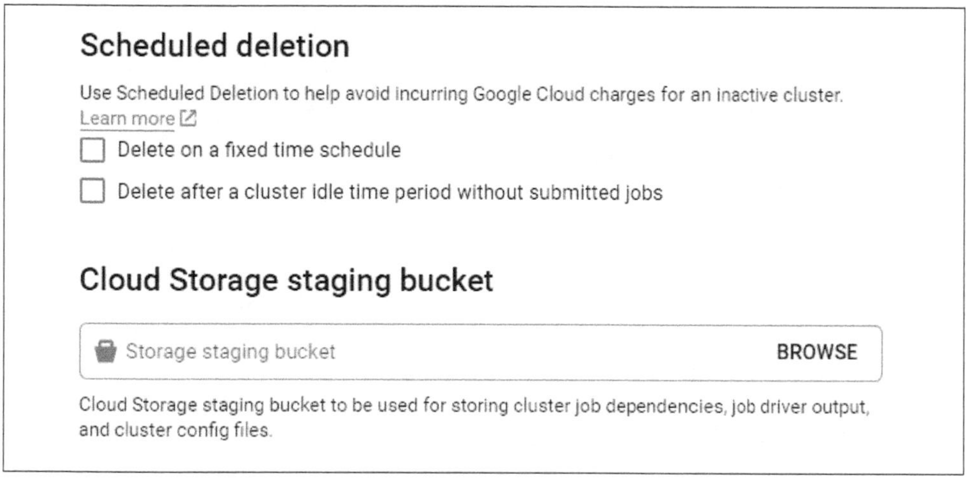

Scheduled deletion

Use Scheduled Deletion to help avoid incurring Google Cloud charges for an inactive cluster.
Learn more ☑

☐ Delete on a fixed time schedule

☐ Delete after a cluster idle time period without submitted jobs

Cloud Storage staging bucket

🪣 Storage staging bucket   BROWSE

Cloud Storage staging bucket to be used for storing cluster job dependencies, job driver output, and cluster config files.

Figure 8-12. Customize cluster—deletion and staging bucket

Finally, click Create to instruct GCP to create the cluster for you. This will take a few moments.

Configuring a Dataproc Cluster

Once the basic cluster is up and running, we can connect to it by clicking on the cluster name and then selecting Jupyter from the Web Interfaces section shown in Figure 8-13.

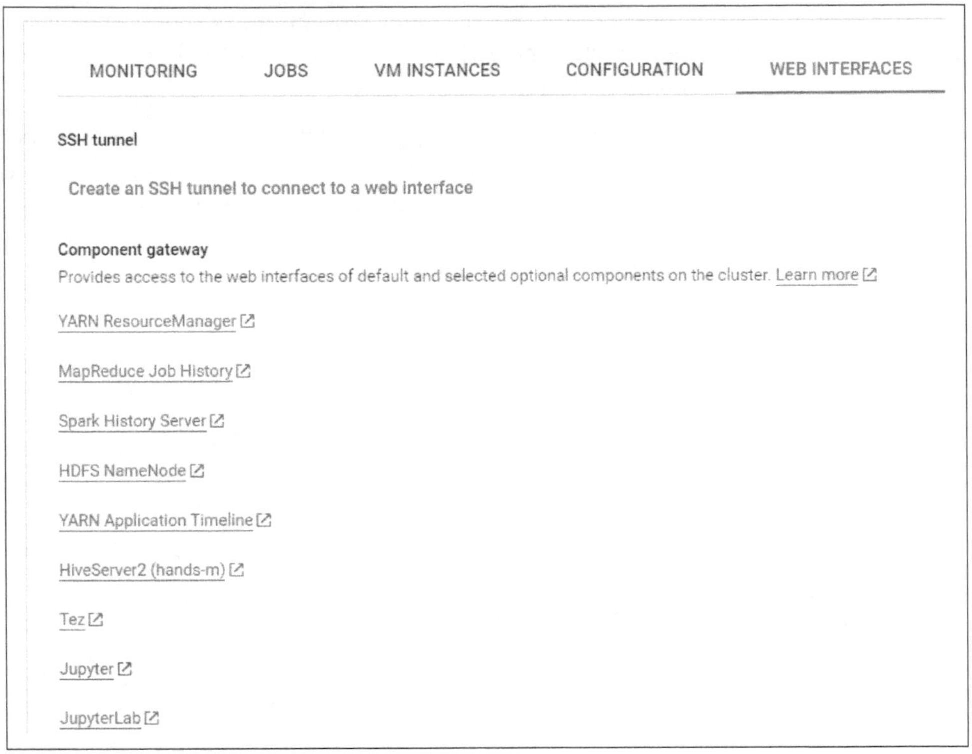

| MONITORING | JOBS | VM INSTANCES | CONFIGURATION | WEB INTERFACES |

SSH tunnel

Create an SSH tunnel to connect to a web interface

Component gateway

Provides access to the web interfaces of default and selected optional components on the cluster. Learn more ⎘

YARN ResourceManager ⎘

MapReduce Job History ⎘

Spark History Server ⎘

HDFS NameNode ⎘

YARN Application Timeline ⎘

HiveServer2 (hands-m) ⎘

Tez ⎘

Jupyter ⎘

JupyterLab ⎘

Figure 8-13. Cluster web interfaces—Jupyter

This will launch a familiar Jupyter environment in a new browser window.

Our next task is to download and configure the software and data we need. From the New menu, select Terminal to bring up a command prompt in a second browser window. Switch to the home directory:

```
>>>cd /home
```

Then clone the repository from the GitHub repo and switch into the newly created directory:

```
>>>git clone https://github.com/mshearer0/handsonentityresolution
```

```
>>>cd handsonentityresolution
```

Next, return to the Jupyter environment and open the *Chapter6.ipynb* notebook. Run the data acquisition and standardization sections of the notebook to re-create the clean Mari and Basic datasets.

Edit the "Saving to Local Storage" section to save the files to:

```
df_c.to_csv('/home/handsonentityresolution/basic_clean.csv')

df_m.to_csv('/home/handsonentityresolution/mari_clean.csv',
    index=False)
```

Now that we have reconstructed our datasets, we need to copy them to the Cloud Storage bucket we created earlier so that they are accessible to all the nodes in our cluster. We do this at the terminal with:

```
>>>gsutil cp /home/handsonentityresolution/* gs://<your
    bucket>/handsonentityresolution/
```

 Note: Remember to substitute your bucket name!

This will create the directory *handsonentityresolution* in your bucket and copy the GitHub repository files across. You'll need these for this chapter and the next one.

Next we need to install Splink:

```
>>>pip install splink
```

Previously, we relied on the approximate string matching functions, like Jaro-Winkler, that were built into DuckDB. These routines aren't available by default in Spark, so we need to download and install a Java ARchive (JAR) file containing these user-defined functions (UDFs) that Splink will call:

```
>>>wget https://github.com/moj-analytical-services/
    splink_scalaudfs/raw/spark3_x/jars/scala-udf-similarity-
    0.1.1_spark3.x.jar
```

Again, we copy this file into our bucket so that these functions are available to the cluster worker nodes:

```
>>>gsutil cp /home/handsonentityresolution/*.jar
    gs://<your bucket>/handsonentityresolution/
```

To tell our cluster where to pick up this file on startup, we need to browse to the *spark-defaults.conf* file in Jupyter at path */Local Disk/etc/spark/conf.dist/* and add the following line, remembering to substitute your bucket name:

```
spark.jars=gs://<your_bucket>/handsonentityresolution/
    scala-udf-similarity-0.1.1_spark3.x.jar
```

To activate this file you need to close your Jupyter windows, return to the cluster menu, and then STOP and START your cluster.

Entity Resolution on Spark

Finally, we are ready to begin our matching process. Open *Chapter8.ipynb* in Jupyter Notebook.

To begin, we load the data files that we saved to our bucket earlier into pandas DataFrames:

```
df_m = pd.read_csv('gs://<your bucket>/
    handsonentityresolution/mari_clean.csv')
df_c = pd.read_csv('gs://<your bucket>/
    handsonentityresolution/basic_clean.csv')
```

Next we configure our Splink settings. These are a little different from the settings we used with the DuckDB backend:

```
from pyspark import SparkContext, SparkConf
from pyspark.sql import SparkSession
from pyspark.sql import types

conf = SparkConf()
conf.set("spark.default.parallelism", "240")
conf.set("spark.sql.shuffle.partitions", "240")

sc = SparkContext.getOrCreate(conf=conf)
spark = SparkSession(sc)
spark.sparkContext.setCheckpointDir("gs://<your bucket>/
    handsonentityresolution/")

spark.udfspark.udf.registerJavaFunction(
    "jaro_winkler_similarity",
    "uk.gov.moj.dash.linkage.JaroWinklerSimilarity",
    types.DoubleType())
```

First, we import `pyspark` functions that allow us to create a new Spark session from Python. Next, we set the configuration parameters to define the amount of parallel processing we want. Then we create the `SparkSession` and set a `Checkpoint` directory that Spark uses as a temporary store.

Lastly, we register a new Java function so that Splink can pick up the Jaro-Winkler similarity routine from the JAR file we set up earlier.

Next we need to set up a Spark schema that we can map our data onto:

```
from pyspark.sql.types import StructType, StructField, StringType, IntegerType

schema = StructType(
    [StructField("Postcode", StringType()),
     StructField("CompanyName", StringType()),
     StructField("unique_id", IntegerType())]
)
```

Then we can create Spark DataFrames (`dfs`) from the pandas DataFrames (`df`) and the schema we have just defined. As both datasets have the same structure, we can use the same schema:

```
dfs_m = spark.createDataFrame(df_m, schema)
dfs_c = spark.createDataFrame(df_c, schema)
```

Our next step is to configure Splink. These settings are the same as we used in Chapter 6:

```
import splink.spark.comparison_library as cl

settings = {
    "link_type": "link_only",
    "blocking_rules_to_generate_predictions": [ "l.Postcode = r.Postcode",
    "l.CompanyName = r.CompanyName", ],
    "comparisons": [ cl.jaro_winkler_at_thresholds("CompanyName",[0.9,0.8]), ],
    "retain_intermediate_calculation_columns" : True,
    "retain_matching_columns" : True
}
```

Then we set up a `SparkLinker` using the Spark DataFrames and settings we have created:

```
from splink.spark.linker import SparkLinker
linker = SparkLinker([dfs_m, dfs_c], settings, input_table_aliases=
["dfs_m", "dfs_c"])
```

As in Chapter 6, we train the *u* and *m* values using random sampling and the expectation-maximization algorithm, respectively:

```
linker.estimate_u_using_random_sampling(max_pairs=5e7)
linker.estimate_parameters_using_expectation_maximisation
    ("l.Postcode = r.Postcode")
```

This is where we begin to see the benefit of switching to Spark. Whereas model training previously took over an hour, now it is completed in only a few minutes.

Alternatively, you can load a pretrained model, *Chapter8_Splink_Settings.json,* from the repository:

```
linker.load_model("<your_path>/Chapter8_Splink_Settings.json")
```

We can then run our predictions and get our results:

```
df_pred = linker.predict(threshold_match_probability=0.1)
    .as_pandas_dataframe()
len(df_pred)
```

Measuring Performance

As expected, switching to Spark doesn't substantially change our results. At a 0.1 match threshold we have 192 matches. Our results are shown in Table 8-1.

Table 8-1. MCA match results (Spark)—low threshold

Match threshold = 0.1	Number of matches	Unique entities matched
Name and postcode match	47	45
Name match only	37	31
Postcode match only	108	27
Total matches	**192**	**85 (deduped)**
Unmatched		11 (of which 2 dissolved)
Total organizations		**96**

This gives a slight improvement in precision and accuracy, due to slight variation in the calculated model parameters.

Tidy Up!

To ensure you aren't charged for continuing to run the virtual machines and their disks, make sure you *DELETE your cluster (not just STOP, which will continue to accrue disk fees) from the Cluster menu.*

You may wish to retain the files in your Cloud Storage bucket for use in the following chapter. However, make sure to delete any staging or temporary buckets if these have been created, as shown in Figure 8-14.

Figure 8-14. Delete staging and temporary buckets

Summary

In this chapter, we learned how to scale up our entity resolution process to run on multiple machines. This gives us the ability to match larger datasets than we could cope with on a single machine, or in a reasonable execution timeframe.

Along the way we've seen how to use Google Cloud Platform to provision compute and storage resources that we can use on demand and pay only for the bandwidth we need.

We've also seen that even with a relatively straightforward example there is a large amount of configuration work we need to do before we can run our entity resolution process. In the next chapter, we will take a look at how the cloud providers provide APIs that offer to abstract away much of this complexity.

Cloud Entity Resolution Services

In the last chapter, we saw how to scale up our entity resolution process to run on a Google Cloud–managed Spark cluster. This approach allowed us to match larger datasets in a reasonable time but it required us to do quite a bit of setup and management ourselves.

An alternative approach is to use entity resolution API provided by a cloud provider to perform the hard work for us. Google, Amazon, and Microsoft all offer these services.

In this chapter, we will use the entity reconciliation service, provided as part of Google's Enterprise Knowledge Graph API, to resolve the MCA and Companies House datasets we examined in Chapters 6 and 8. We will:

- Upload our standardized datasets to Google's data warehouse, BigQuery.
- Provide a mapping of our data schema to a standard ontology.
- Invoke the API from the console (we will also invoke the API using a Python script).
- Use some basic SQL to process the results.

To complete the chapter we will examine how well the service performs.

Introduction to BigQuery

BigQuery is Google's fully managed, serverless data warehouse that enables scalable analysis over petabytes of data. It is a platform as a service that supports data querying and analysis using a dialect of SQL.

To begin, we select the BigQuery product from the Google Cloud console. Under ANALYSIS we select "SQL workspace."

Our first step is to select "Create dataset" from the ellipsis menu alongside your project name, as shown in Figure 9-1.

Figure 9-1. BigQuery Create dataset

In the pop-up window, as shown in Figure 9-2, we need to name the Dataset ID as Chapter9, and then select a Location Type. You can then select a specific Region if you prefer or simply accept the Multi-region default. Optionally, you can add a number of days after which the table expires automatically.

Once we have an empty dataset created, our next task is to upload our MCA and Companies House tables. We can upload these tables from the data we saved in the Google Cloud Storage bucket in Chapter 8.

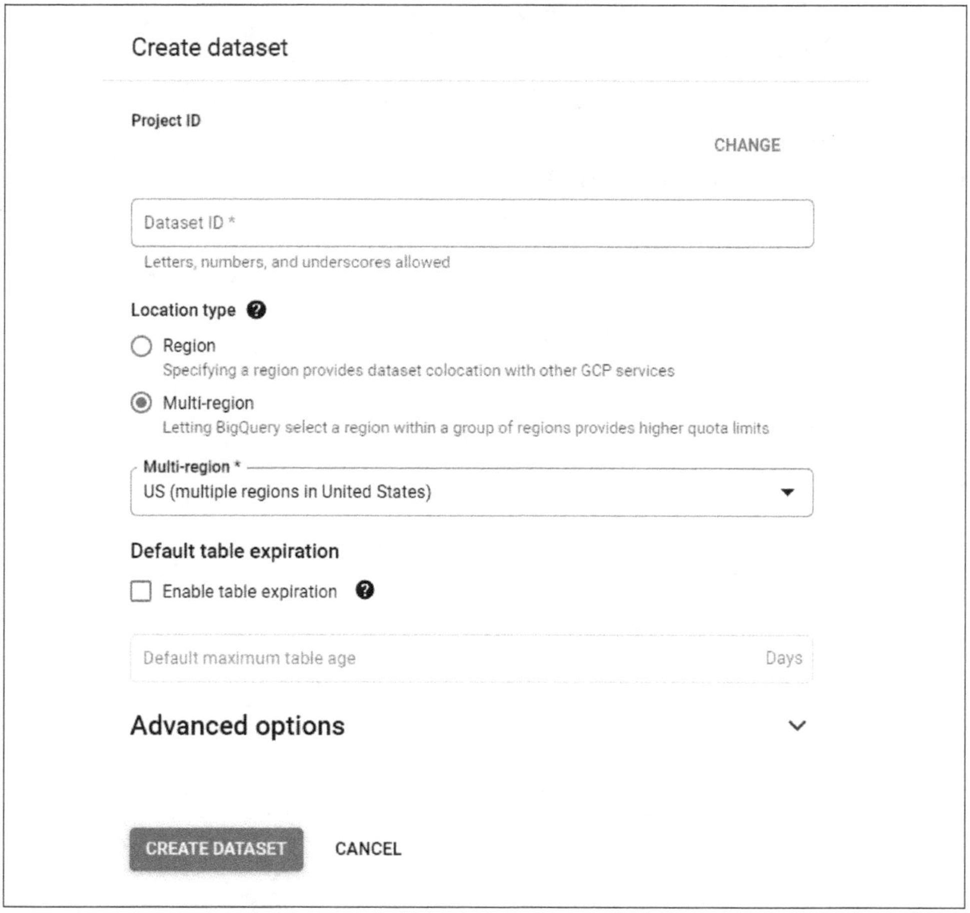

Figure 9-2. BigQuery Create dataset config

With the dataset selected, we can click "+ Add," or Add Data and then select Google Cloud Storage as the source (as shown in Figure 9-3). You can then browse to your Cloud Storage bucket and select the *mari_clean.csv* file. Select the Chapter9 dataset as the destination and name the table *mari*. Under Schema, click the "Auto detect" checkbox. You can accept the remainder of the default settings.

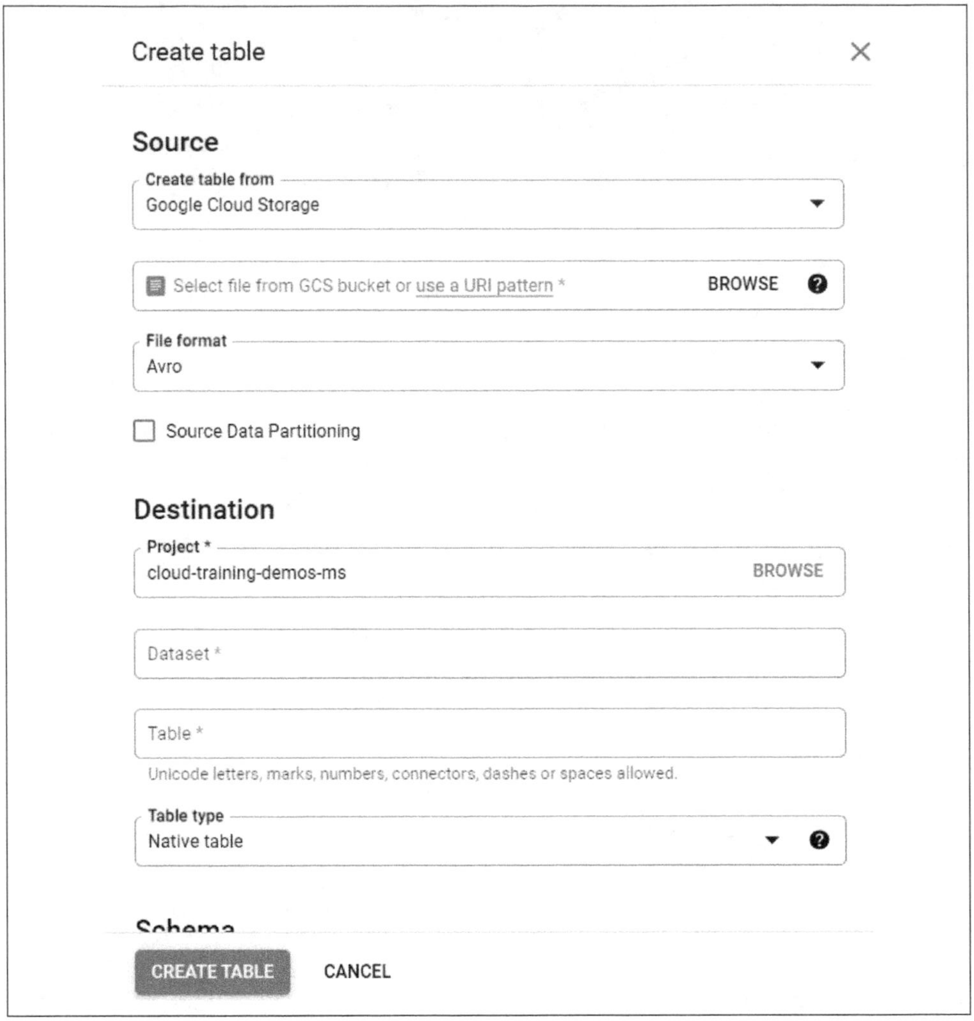

Figure 9-3. BigQuery Create table

Repeat this procedure for the *basic_clean.csv* file, naming it *basic*. You can then select the table from the dataset to examine the schema. Selecting Preview will give you a view of the first few rows, as shown in Figure 9-4.

Figure 9-4. BigQuery table schema

Now that we have successfully loaded our data, we need to tell the Enterprise Knowledge Graph API how to map our schema and then run a reconciliation job.

Enterprise Knowledge Graph API

The Google Enterprise Knowledge Graph API provides a lightweight entity resolution service that they call Entity Reconciliation. The service uses an AI model trained on Google data. It uses a parallel version of *hierarchical agglomerative clustering*.

Hierarchical Agglomerative Clustering

This is a "bottom-up" approach to clustering entities. Each entity starts in its own cluster and then they are aggregated depending upon their similarity.

At the time of writing, the Entity Reconciliation service is at Preview status and is made available on Pre-GA terms, details of which are available on the Google Cloud website (*https://oreil.ly/dThBk*).

To enable the API, select Enterprise KG under Artificial Intelligence from the console navigation menu. From here you can click "Enable the Enterprise Knowledge Graph API" for your project.

Schema Mapping

To set up our entity resolution job, we first need to map our data schema onto the schema that the Google Entity Reconciliation API understands. We do this by creating a mapping file for each data source we are going to use. The API uses a human-readable simple format language called YARRRML to define the mappings between source schema and a target ontology from schema.org. It supports three different entity types: Organization, Person, and Local Business. For our example, we will use the Organization schema.

To begin, we click on Schema Mapping and then select "Create a Mapping" in the Organization box. This brings us to an editor where we can modify and save a template mapping file. The mapping file is divided into a prefix section that tells the API which model and schema reference we are going to use. The mapping section then lists each entity type contained in the dataset. For each entity type, we specify the sources, a subject key (s) that uniquely refers to an entity in the dataset, and then the predicate list (po) which specifies the attributes of the entity we wish to match on.

The default template is as follows:

```
prefixes:
  ekg: http://cloud.google.com/ekg/0.0.1#
  schema: https://schema.org/

mappings:
  organization:
    sources:
      - [example_project:example_dataset.example_table~bigquery]
    s: ekg:company_$(record_id)
    po:
      - [a, schema:Organization]
      - [schema:name, $(company_name_in_source)]
      - [schema:streetAddress, $(street)]
      - [schema:postalCode, $(postal_code)]
      - [schema:addressCountry, $(country)]
      - [schema:addressLocality, $(city)]
      - [schema:addressRegion, $(state)]
      - [ekg:recon.source_name, $(source_system)]
      - [ekg:recon.source_key, $(source_key)]
```

Starting with the mapping file for the MCA dataset, edit the default template as follows, remembering to insert your project name in the source line. This file is also available in the repository as *Chapter9SchemaMari*:

```
prefixes:
  ekg: http://cloud.google.com/ekg/0.0.1#
  schema: https://schema.org/

mappings:
  organization:
    sources:
      - [<your_project_name>:Chapter9.mari~bigquery]
    s: ekg:company1_$(unique_id)
    po:
      - [a, schema:Organization]
      - [schema:postalCode, $(Postcode)]
      - [schema:name, $(CompanyName)]
      - [ekg:recon.source_name, (mari)]
      - [ekg:recon.source_key, $(unique_id)]
```

Note here that we are pointing the API to the *mari* BigQuery table we created earlier in the Chapter9 dataset. We are using the `unique_id` column as our subject key, and we are mapping our `Postcode` field to the `postalCode` property in the schema and our `CompanyName` field to the `name` property.

Save this edited file into your Google Storage bucket under the *handsonentityresolution* directory as:

```
gs://<your bucket>/handsonentityresolution/Chapter9SchemaMari
```

Repeat this process to create a mapping file for the Companies House dataset, saving in the same location as *Chapter9SchemaBasic*. Remember to substitute *basic* for *mari* in the relevant lines and reference these entities as *company2*:

```
  - [<your_bucket>:Chapter9.basic~bigquery]
s: ekg:company2_$(unique_id)
po:
    - [a, schema:Organization]
    - [ekg:recon.source_name, (basic)]
```

We now have our datasets and our mapping files, so we can run an entity resolution (or reconciliation) job.

Reconciliation Job

To start a reconciliation job, select Jobs from the Enterprise KG section in the console navigation menu, as shown in Figure 9-5.

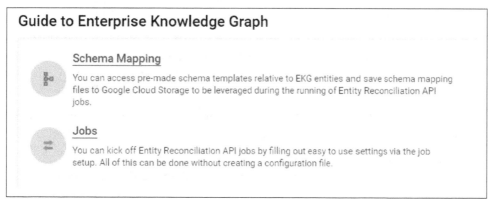

Figure 9-5. Start a reconciliation job

Select the RUN A JOB tab, as shown in Figure 9-6.

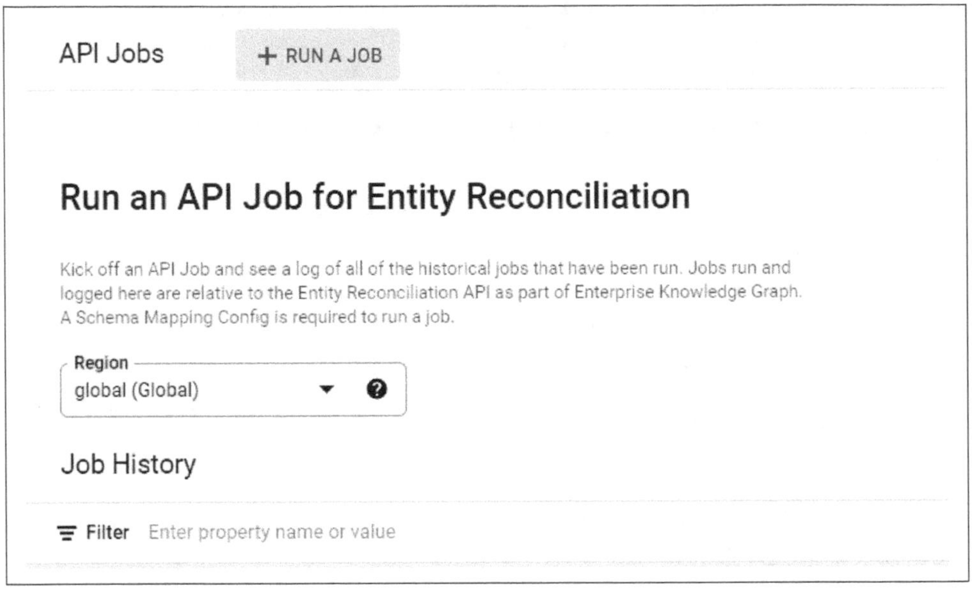

API Jobs   **+ RUN A JOB**

Run an API Job for Entity Reconciliation

Kick off an API Job and see a log of all of the historical jobs that have been run. Jobs run and logged here are relative to the Entity Reconciliation API as part of Enterprise Knowledge Graph. A Schema Mapping Config is required to run a job.

Region
global (Global)   ▼   ❓

Job History

☰ Filter   Enter property name or value

Figure 9-6. Run an API Job for Entity Reconciliation

From the pop-up menu:

Step 1: Click "Select entity type"
Select Organization.

Step 2: Add BigQuery data sources
Browse to the BigQuery path and select the *mari* table. Then select the matching mapping table by browsing to the *handsonentityresolution* directory in your bucket and selecting the *Chapter9SchemaMari* file we created earlier.

Click Add Another BigQuery Datasource and repeat the process for the *basic* table and mapping file.

Step 3: Set BigQuery data destination
Browse and select the Chapter9 BigQuery dataset to tell the API where to write its results.

Step 4: Advanced settings (optional)
For the final step, we can specify a previous result table so that the entity reconciliation service assigns consistent IDs to entities across different jobs, as shown in Figure 9-7. This can be particularly useful to update existing entity records as new data is added.

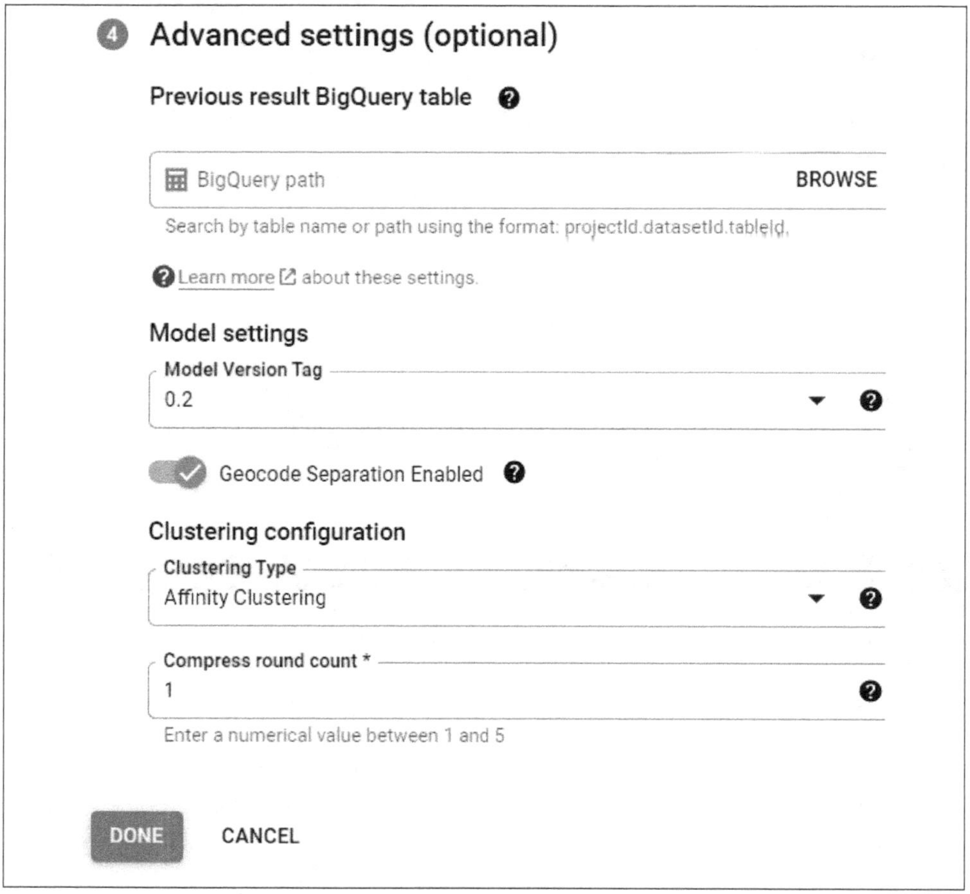

Figure 9-7. Entity Reconciliation API advanced settings

The number of clustering rounds (iterations of the entity resolution model) can be specified; the higher the number, the more loosely entities are merged into the same cluster. The default is fine for our use case.

Finally, we can click Done and start our job. Assuming all is well, we should then see a new job created under Job History, as shown in Figure 9-8.

Job History

Filter Enter property name or value

Job resource name	Status	Elapsed time	Entity type
15719257497877843494	⟳ Knowledge extraction	22 sec	Organization

Figure 9-8. Entity Reconciliation Job History

We can watch the Job Display Status column to monitor the progress of our job as it moves sequentially through the display states shown in Table 9-1, and then finally displays Finished when complete.

Table 9-1. Job display state

Job display state	Code state	Description
Running	JOB_STATE_RUNNING	The job is in progress.
Knowledge extraction	JOB_STATE_KNOWLEDGE_EXTRACTION	Enterprise Knowledge Graph is pulling data out from BigQuery and creating features.
Reconciliation preprocessing	JOB_STATE_RECON_PREPROCESSING	The job is at the reconciliation preprocessing step.
Clustering	JOB_STATE_CLUSTERING	The job is at the clustering step.
Exporting clusters	JOB_STATE_EXPORTING_CLUSTERS	The job is writing output into the BigQuery destination dataset.

This job should take approximately 1 hour 20 minutes but the duration varies widely at this Preview stage of the product.

When the job is finished, if we look in the BigQuery SQL workspace we should see a new table in our Chapter9 dataset called something like clusters_15719257497877843494, as shown in Figure 9-9.

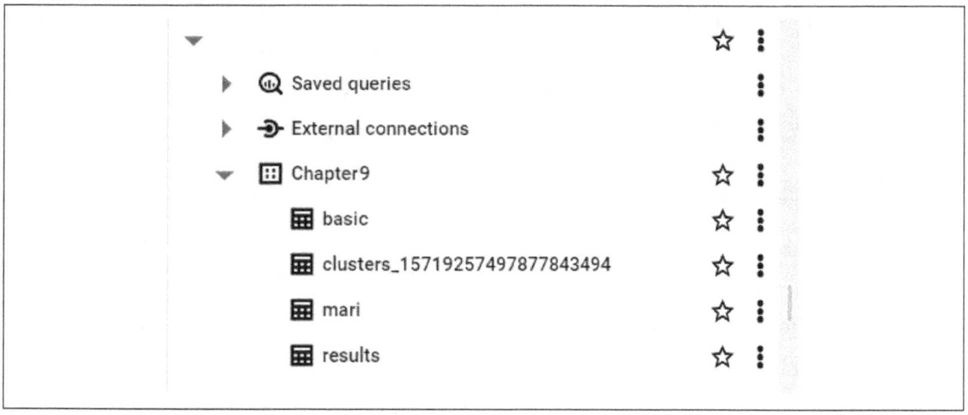

Figure 9-9. BigQuery clusters results table

Selecting the clusters_15719257497877843494 table and then selecting the Preview tab gives us a view of the results. Figure 9-10 shows the first few rows.

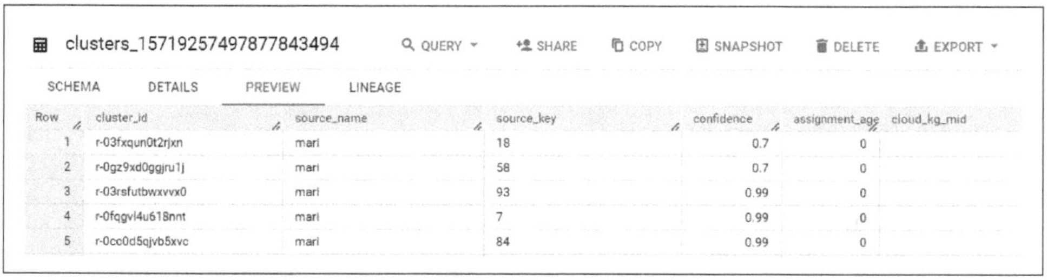

Row	cluster_id	source_name	source_key	confidence	assignment_age	cloud_kg_mid
1	r-03fxqun0t2rjxn	mari	18	0.7	0	
2	r-0gz9xd0ggjru1j	mari	58	0.7	0	
3	r-03rsfutbwxvvx0	mari	93	0.99	0	
4	r-0fqgvl4u618nnt	mari	7	0.99	0	
5	r-0cc0d5qjvb5xvc	mari	84	0.99	0	

Figure 9-10. BigQuery cluster results preview

Let's consider the columns in the output:

- The *cluster_id* gives the unique reference of the cluster to which the Entity Reconciliation API has assigned the source entity.
- The *source_name* column gives us the name of the source table, in our case either *mari* or *basic*.
- The *source_key* column contains the `unique_id` of the row in the source table.
- The *confidence* score, between 0 and 1, indicates how strongly a record is associated with a given cluster.
- The *assignment_age* column is an internal API reference.
- The *cloud_kg_mid* column contains an MID value link to the entity in the Google Cloud Enterprise Knowledge Graph if the API can resolve a match. This can be used to look up additional details that Google has on the entity using the Cloud Enterprise Knowledge Graph API.

As every entity in both the *mari* and *basic* tables is assigned to a cluster, the row count for this table is the sum of the row counts for the source tables. In our case, this is over 5 million rows. At a glance, it's not easy to identify which entities the API has matched, so we need to refine this data a little.

Result Processing

With our entity reconciliation results we can then use BigQuery SQL to process this raw information into an easier form for us to examine the resolved entities.

To start, we click "Compose a New Query", which takes us to a SQL editor. You can cut and paste the SQL template from the *Chapter9.sql* file.

First we need to create a temporary table containing only rows whose cluster_id has at least one MCA match. We do this by building a subset of the cluster table whose rows have "mari" as the source_name. Then we find the intersection between the rows of this subset and the rows of the full cluster table using an INNER JOIN on matching cluster_ids.

Make sure to replace the cluster table name with the name of your results table, which will be in the format clusters_<job reference>:

```
CREATE TEMP TABLE temp AS SELECT
    src.* FROM Chapter9.clusters_15719257497877843494 AS src
        INNER JOIN (SELECT cluster_id from
            Chapter9.clusters_15719257497877843494 WHERE
                source_name = "mari") AS mari
            ON src.cluster_id = mari.cluster_id;
```

The resulting temporary table now has only 151 rows. Next we create a second temporary table, this time with the subset of clusters that have both an MCA match and at least one Companies House match; i.e., we remove clusters with only an MCA match.

To do this we select those cluster_ids with a count of greater than 1 and again find the intersection of this subset with the first temporary table using an INNER JOIN on the matching cluster_ids.

Now we have a table of clusters containing only rows where the entity is found in both the Companies House and MCA datasets:

```
CREATE TEMP TABLE match AS SELECT
    src.* FROM temp AS src
        INNER JOIN (SELECT cluster_id FROM temp GROUP BY cluster_id
            HAVING COUNT(*) > 1) AS matches
        ON matches.cluster_id = src.cluster_id;
```

This table now has 106 rows. We have the population we are looking for, so we can create a persistent results table picking up the `CompanyName` and `Postcode` from the source tables so that we can examine the results.

We need to build this table in two parts. First, for the rows that refer to the Companies House data we need to look up the identifier in the `source_key` column and use that to retrieve the corresponding name and postcode. Then we need to do the same for rows that refer to the MCA data. We use the `UNION ALL` statement to join these two datasets and then `ORDER BY confidence` first and then `cluster_id`. This means that entities assigned to the same cluster are adjacent in the table for easy viewing:

```
CREATE TABLE Chapter9.results AS

    SELECT * FROM Chapter9.basic AS bas
    INNER JOIN (SELECT * FROM match WHERE match.source_name = "basic") AS res1
    ON res1.source_key = CAST(bas.unique_id AS STRING)


    UNION ALL


    SELECT * FROM Chapter9.mari AS mari
        INNER JOIN (SELECT * FROM match WHERE match.source_name = "mari") AS res2
        ON res2.source_key = CAST(mari.unique_id AS STRING)

    ORDER BY confidence, cluster_id
```

This gives us our results table, which looks like that given in Figure 9-11.

Row	Postcode	CompanyName	unique_id	cluster_id	source_name	source_key	confidence
1	BS31 1TP	CREW AND CONCIERGE	18	r-03fxqun0t2rjxn	mari	18	0.7
2	BS31 1TP	CREW & CONCIERGE	1182534	r-03fxqun0t2rjxn	basic	1182534	0.7
3	CO3 8PH	C POWER ENERGY	10	r-0b5ym0g32sbupp	mari	10	0.7
4	CO3 8PH	CPOWER ENERGY	1163854	r-0b5ym0g32sbupp	basic	1163854	0.7
5	SO45 1TA	SEAMARINER	70	r-0c30r6v43urcn4	mari	70	0.7
6	SO45 1DD	SEAMARINER	4197604	r-0c30r6v43urcn4	basic	4197604	0.7
7	PO6 4PR	ADVANCED RESOURCE MANA...	189059	r-0czcb444y39b4j	basic	189059	0.7
8	PO6 4PR	ADVANCED RESOURCE MANA...	189060	r-0czcb444y39b4j	basic	189060	0.7
9	HU10 7WG	CP MARINE	17	r-0fxwtpzqvw7r6u	mari	17	0.7
10	HU10 7LA	C P MARINE	834944	r-0fxwtpzqvw7r6u	basic	834944	0.7
11	G81 2QR	NORTHERN MARINE MANNIN...	58	r-0gz9xd0ggjru1j	mari	58	0.7
12	G81 2QR	NORTHERN MARINE MANNING	3410320	r-0gz9xd0ggjru1j	basic	3410320	0.7
13	PO6 4PR	ADVANCED RESOURCE MANA...	3	r-0czcb444y39b4j	mari	3	0.8
14	PO6 4PR	ADVANCED RESOURCE MANA...	189061	r-0czcb444y39b4j	basic	189061	0.8

Figure 9-11. Processed results table

In the first row, we can see that both the MCA entity with `CompanyName` CREW AND CONCIERGE, `Postcode` BS31 1TP, and `unique_id` 18 has been assigned to cluster r-03fxqun0t2rjxn. In the second row, the Companies House entity with `CompanyName`

CREW and CONCIERGE, the same `Postcode`, and `unique_id` 1182534 has been assigned to the same cluster.

This means the Google Entity Reconciliation API has grouped these records into the same cluster, i.e., resolved these rows as referring to the same real-world entity, with a confidence rating of 0.7.

Before we examine these results in detail, we'll take a quick detour to see how to invoke the API from Python instead of the cloud console.

Entity Reconciliation Python Client

The Google Enterprise Knowledge Graph API also supports a Python client to create, cancel, and delete entity reconciliation jobs. We can use the Cloud Shell virtual machine to run these Python scripts and launch these jobs.

Google Cloud Shell

Cloud Shell provisions a Compute Engine virtual machine running a Debian-based Linux OS for temporary use. The instance persists while your Cloud Shell session is active; after an hour of inactivity, your session terminates and its virtual machine is discarded. Cloud Shell provisions 5 GB of free persistent disk storage.

To activate Google Cloud Shell, click on the terminal symbol in the top right of the console. This will open a window with a command-line prompt.

A Python script to invoke the entity reconciliation job is included in the repository. To transfer a copy to your Cloud Shell machine we can use:

```
>>>gsutil cp gs://<your_bucket>/handsonentityresolution/
    Chapter9.py .
```

A pop-up window will ask you to authorize the Cloud Shell to connect to your bucket.

The script, *Chapter9.py*, is reproduced here. You can use the Cloud Shell editor to edit this file to reference your project and bucket:

```
#!/usr/bin/env python
# coding: utf-8

from google.cloud import enterpriseknowledgegraph as ekg

project_id = '<your_project>'
dataset_id = 'Chapter9'

import google.cloud.enterpriseknowledgegraph as ekg
```

```
client = ekg.EnterpriseKnowledgeGraphServiceClient()
parent = client.common_location_path(project=project_id, location='global')

input_config = ekg.InputConfig(
        bigquery_input_configs=[
            ekg.BigQueryInputConfig(
                bigquery_table=client.table_path(
                    project=project_id, dataset=dataset_id, table='mari'
                ),
                gcs_uri='gs://<your bucket>/
                    handsonentityresolution/Chapter9SchemaMari',
            ),
             ekg.BigQueryInputConfig(
                bigquery_table=client.table_path(
                    project=project_id, dataset=dataset_id, table='basic'
                ),
                gcs_uri='gs://<your bucket>/
                    handsonentityresolution/Chapter9SchemaBasic',
            )
        ],
        entity_type=ekg.InputConfig.EntityType.ORGANIZATION,
    )

output_config = ekg.OutputConfig(
        bigquery_dataset=client.dataset_path(project=project_id,
            dataset=dataset_id)
    )

entity_reconciliation_job = ekg.EntityReconciliationJob(
        input_config=input_config, output_config=output_config
)

request = ekg.CreateEntityReconciliationJobRequest(
        parent=parent, entity_reconciliation_job=entity_reconciliation_job
)

response = client.create_entity_reconciliation_job(request=request)

print(f"Job: {response.name}")
```

The Cloud Shell has Python installed so we can simply run this script from the command prompt with the following:

```
>>>python Chapter9.py
```

To process the results, we can use the SQL script we examined previously. To copy this from your Cloud Storage bucket:

```
>>>gsutil cp gs://<your_bucket>/handsonentityresolution/
    Chapter9.sql
```

Then we run this BigQuery script using:

```
>>>bq query --use_legacy_sql=false < Chapter9.sql
```

Note that if the results table has already been created by running this query from the SQL workspace, this command will fail because the table already exists. You can delete the table using:

```
>>>bq rm -f -t Chapter9.results
```

Now we can examine how well the API performed on our example.

Measuring Performance

Recall from our Preview of the BigQuery results table that we have 106 rows. The distribution of match confidence is shown in Table 9-2.

Table 9-2. Match confidence

Number of matches	Confidence
6	0.7
1	0.8
45	0.99
44	No match found

Two of the MCA entities matched to two of the Companies House entities.

Looking back to Figure 9-11, we can see the first seven matches in ascending order of confidence. You can see that the entity reconciliation service has been able to match these entities in spite of minor spelling differences or postcode variations. The remainder are exact matches on both CompanyName and Postcode with the exception of a mismatched hyphen between INDIE PEARL and INDIE-PEARL, which has not affected the confidence score.

If we assume that the unique matches are true positive matches and that the two additional matches are false positives, then we can evaluate our performance as:

$$True\ positive\ matches\,(TP) = 52$$

$$False\ positive\ matches\,(FP) = 2$$

$$False\ negative\ matches\,(FN) = 44$$

$$Precision = \frac{TP}{(TP+FP)} = \frac{52}{(52+2)} \approx 96\,\%$$

$$Recall = \frac{TP}{(TP+FN)} = \frac{52}{(52+44)} \approx 54.2\,\%$$

So the entity reconciliation gives us excellent precision but with relatively poor recall.

Summary

In this chapter we have seen how to use the Google Cloud Entity Reconciliation API to resolve our organization entities. We have seen how to configure and run matching jobs from both the cloud console and via the Python client.

Using the API abstracts us away from much of the complexity of configuring our own matching process. It is also inherently scalable to very large datasets (hundreds of millions of rows). However, we are constrained to using a set of predefined schemas and we don't have the freedom to tune the matching algorithm to optimize the recall/precision trade-off for our use case.

CHAPTER 10

Privacy-Preserving Record Linkage

In previous chapters, we have seen how to resolve entities via exact and probabilistic matching techniques, using both local compute and cloud-based solutions. The first step in these matching processes is to assemble the data sources onto a single platform for comparison. Where the data sources to be resolved share a common owner, or can be freely shared in their entirety for the purposes of matching, then centralized processing is the most efficient approach.

However, data sources can often be sensitive, and privacy considerations may preclude unrestricted sharing with another party. This chapter considers how privacy-preserving record linkage techniques can be used to perform basic entity resolution across data sources held separately by two parties. In particular, we will consider private set intersection as a practical means to identify entities known to both parties without either side disclosing their full dataset to the other.

An Introduction to Private Set Intersection

Private set intersection (PSI) is a cryptographic technique that allows the intersection between two overlapping sets of information, held by two different parties, to be identified without revealing the nonintersecting elements to either counterparty.

For example, as shown in Figure 10-1, the intersection between Set A, owned by Alice, and Set B, owned by Bob, can be identified as comprising elements 4 and 5 without revealing Bob's knowledge of entities 6, 7, or 8 to Alice or Alice's knowledge of 1, 2, or 3 to Bob.

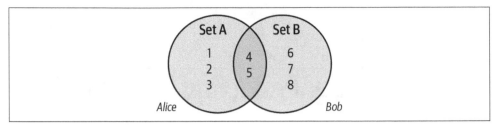

Figure 10-1. Private set intersection

Once this intersection is known, we can combine the information held by both Alice and Bob about resolved entities 4 and 5 to allow us to make better decisions about how to handle these entities. This technique is commonly applied in a single direction, say between Alice (acting as a client) and Bob (acting as a server), where Alice learns the intersecting elements but Bob learns nothing about Alice's dataset.

Example Use Case for PSI

A financial institution in a privacy jurisdiction might wish to see whether any of its customers are shared with another organization without revealing the identity of its customers. The sharing organization is willing to disclose the individuals they have in common but is not willing to divulge its full customer list.

This is the approach we will examine in this chapter, where the sets of information are lists of entities held by both parties, and the client is trying to establish whether the server holds information on an entity in their set without revealing any of their entities in the process. This perhaps sounds like magic, but bear with me!

How PSI Works

In a client/server setting where the server is happy to share its dataset with the client, the simplest solution for the client to discover the intersection is simply for the server to send a full copy of its dataset to the client, who can then perform the matching process in private. The client learns which matching elements are also held by the server and can build a fuller picture of the common entities while the server learns nothing.

In practice, this full disclosure approach is often not possible, either because the size of the server dataset exceeds the capacity of the client device or because while the server is willing to reveal the existence of, and information describing, the intersecting elements it has in common with the client, it is not willing or permitted to divulge the entire set.

If full sharing from server to client is not possible, then a commonly proposed solution, often referred to as *naive PSI*, is for both parties to apply the same mapping function to each of the elements in their datasets. The server then shares its transformed values with the client who can compare these processed values with their own equivalents to find the intersection and then look up the corresponding original element using the matching client reference as a key. A *cryptographic hash function* is often used for this purpose.

Cryptographic Hash Functions

A cryptographic hash function is a hash algorithm (a map of an arbitrary binary string to a binary string of a fixed size). SHA-256 is a commonly used cryptographic hash that generates a 256-bit value, known as a digest.

Although efficient, this hash-based approach can potentially be exploited by the client to attempt to discover the full server dataset. One possible attack is for the client to prepare a comprehensive table of original and transformed values, match this inclusive set against all the received server values, and then look up the original values in the table, thereby reconstructing the full server dataset. When a hash function is used to perform the mapping, this precomputed lookup table is called a rainbow table.

For this reason, we will continue our search for a stronger cryptographic solution. Over the years, several different cryptographic techniques have been employed to implement PSI solutions. The first class of algorithms used public key cryptography to secure the exchange so that only the client could decrypt the matching elements and discover the intersection. This approach is highly efficient in the bandwidth required between the client and the server but at the expense of longer runtimes to compute the intersection.

Generic secure computation circuits have also been applied to the PSI problem, as have oblivious transfer techniques. More recently, fully homomorphic encryption schemes have been proposed to enable approximate, as well as exact, matching to take place.

For the purposes of this book, we will consider the original public key technique, proposed by Catherine Meadows in 1986 using the *Elliptic Curve Diffie-Hellman* (ECDH) protocol.[1] We won't delve into the details or the mathematics behind the encryption and decryption process. If you'd like to understand this subject in more

---

1 Meadows, Catherine, "A More Efficient Cryptographic Matchmaking Protocol for Use in the Absence of a Continuously Available Third Party," *1986 IEEE Symposium on Security and Privacy*, Oakland, CA, USA, 1986, pp. 134, *https://doi.org/10.1109/SP.1986.10022*.

detail, I recommend *Learning Digital Identity* by Phillip J. Windley (O'Reilly) as a good primer.

PSI Protocol Based on ECDH

The basic PSI protocol works like this:

1. The client encrypts its data elements, using a commutative encryption scheme, with its secret key.

> ## Commutative Encryption
>
> An encryption algorithm is called commutative if double encryption using two different keys produces a ciphertext that can be correctly decrypted using the keys in arbitrary order.

2. The client sends the server their encrypted elements. This reveals the number of distinct elements in the client dataset but nothing else to the server.

3. The server then further encrypts the client-encrypted values, using a new secret key unique to this request, and sends these values back to the client.

4. The client then exploits the commutative properties of the encryption scheme to allow it to decrypt the all-server elements received from the server, effectively removing the original encryption it applied, but leaving the elements encrypted by the server secret key.

5. The server encrypts all the elements in its dataset using the same scheme and secret key created for this request and sends the encrypted values to the client.

6. The client can then compare the full set of encrypted server elements, received at step 5, with the members of its own set, now encrypted only by the server key from step 4, to determine the intersection.

This protocol is shown in Figure 10-2.

In its basic form, this protocol means that the entire server dataset is sent to the client, in encrypted form, in response to each client query. This volume of data could be prohibitive, in either compute or space requirements. However, we can employ encoding techniques to drastically reduce the volume of data we have to exchange, at the price of introducing a small percentage of false positives. We will consider two techniques: Bloom filters and Golomb-coded sets (GCSs). Simple examples to illustrate the encoding process are provided in *Chapter10GCSBloomExamples.ipynb*.

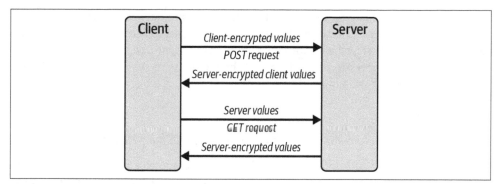

Figure 10-2. PSI protocol

Bloom Filters

Bloom filters are a probabilistic data structure that can very efficiently store, and allow us to confirm, the presence of a data element in a set. An empty Bloom filter is a bit array whose bits are initialized to 0. To add an item to the filter, the data element is processed by a number of hash functions; the output of each maps to a bit position in the filter, which is then set to 1.

To test whether a new data element is in the set, we simply check whether the bit positions corresponding to its hashed values are all set to 1. If they are, then the new element is probably already present in the set. I say probably because it's possible that those bits may have been set independently to represent other values, resulting in a false positive. What we can be sure of though is that if any of the bits are not set to 1, then our new element is not present in the set; i.e., there are no false negatives.

The likelihood of a false positive depends on the length of the filter, the number of hash functions, and the number of elements in the dataset. These can be optimized as:

$$Bloom\ filter\ length\ (bits) = \left\lceil \frac{-max\_elements \times \log_2{(fpr)}}{8 \times \ln 2} \right\rceil \times 8$$

where

$$fpr = false\ positive\ rate$$
$$max\_elements = \max{(num\_client\_inputs, num\_server\_inputs)}$$

and

$$Number\ hash\ functions = \lceil -\log_2{(fpr)} \rceil$$

Using a Bloom filter to encode and return the encrypted server values, as opposed to returning the full set of raw encrypted values, allows us to reduce this set representation to a practical size the client can handle. The client can then apply the same Bloom encoding process to check if any of the elements of its set (encrypted by the server) are present in the filter.

Bloom filter example

Let's progressively build a simple Bloom filter to illustrate the process.

Say we incrementally add decimal values 217, 354, and 466 to a Bloom filter of length 32 bits using 4 hash iterations. Suppose the hash iteration is calculated according to the following:

$$Hash1 = SHA256(Encrypted\ value\ prefixed\ by\ 1)\ \%\ 32$$

$$Hash2 = SHA256(Encrypted\ value\ prefixed\ by\ 2)\ \%\ 32$$

and

$$Hash\ Value = (Hash1 + Iteration\ number \times Hash2)\ \%\ 32$$

then we progressively build the Bloom filter in Table 10-1.

Table 10-1. Bloom filter example

Encrypted value	Hash iteration	Hash value (Range 0-31)	Bloom filter (Positions 0–31, right to left)
Empty filter			00000000000000000000000000000000
217	0	24	00000001000000000000000000000000
	1	19	00000001000010000000000000000000
	2	14	00000001000010000100000000000000
	3	9	00000001000010000100001000000000
354	0	5	00000001000010000100001000100000
	1	4	00000001000010000100001000110000
	2	3	00000001000010000100001000111000
	3	2	00000001000010000100001000111100
466	0	14	00000001000010000100001000111100
	1	18	00000001000011000100001000111100
	2	22	00000001010011000100001000111100
	3	26	00000101010011000100001000111100
Completed filter			00000101010011000100001000111100

Here we can see a collision where the first hash iteration of the third value sets the bit in position 14 to 1, although it's already been set to 1 previously by the third iteration of the first value.

Similarly, if all the bit positions corresponding to the hash iterations for a new value were already set to 1, then it would appear that element was in the dataset when in fact it wasn't. For example, if we want to test if the value decimal 14 is in the server dataset, we compute its hash values as shown in Table 10-2.

Table 10-2. Bloom filter test

Test value	Hash iteration	Hash value (Range 0–31)	Bloom filter (Positions 0–31, right to left)	Bit check
Bloom filter			00000101010011000100001000111100	
14	0	22	00000000001000000000000000000000	True
	1	2	00000000000000000000000000000100	True
	2	14	00000000000000001000000000000000	True
	3	26	00000100000000000000000000000000	True

From this simple example, we would erroneously conclude that the value 14 is in the server data when it isn't. Clearly, a longer Bloom filter length is needed.

Golomb-Coded Sets

Golomb-coded sets (GCS), like Bloom filters, are a probabilistic data structure that can offer an even more efficient way of encoding the presence of elements in a dataset. To construct a GCS representation of a dataset, we first hash the original data elements into a set of hash values within a set range.

The hash range is calculated as:

$$Hash\ range = \frac{max\_elements}{fpr}$$

As before:

$$fpr = false\ positive\ rate$$

$$max\_elements = \max\left(num\_client\_inputs, num\_server\_inputs\right)$$

We then sort these hash values in ascending order and calculate a divisor that represents the geometric range of values. If this divisor is chosen to be a power of 2, then this variant is called Rice encoding and can be calculated from the ascending list as:

$$GCS\_divisor\_power\_of\_2 = \max\left(0, round\left(-log_2\left(-log_2(1.0 - prob)\right)\right)\right)$$

where

$$prob = \frac{1}{avg}$$

$$avg = \frac{(last\_element\_in\_ascending\_list + 1)}{number\_elements\_in\_ascending\_list}$$

Next, we compute the differences between consecutive values, removing any 0-value differences, and divide these delta hash values by 2 to the power of the GCS divisor previously calculated. This division yields a quotient and a remainder. To complete the encoding, we represent the quotient using unary coding and the remainder in binary, padded to the maximum length using 0s.

Unary Coding

Unary coding represents a natural number as a sequence of 1s (or 0s) whose length is equivalent to the number to be represented, followed by a terminating 0 (or 1). A few examples are shown in Table 10-3.

Table 10-3. Examples of unary encoding

Number	Unary with 0s	Unary with 1s
0	1	0
1	01	10
2	001	110
3	0001	1110

For those of us used to looking at binary values, this takes a bit of getting used to.

Each element is encoded in this manner and the bits concatenated together to form the GCS structure. To check for a given element in the structure, we scan through the bits, reconstructing each element in turn from the unary quotient and binary remainder, and then progressively sum the difference values we obtain to reconstruct the original hashed values, which we can compare against the hash of our test value.

As with Bloom filters, there is a possibility of a false positive due to a hash collision, the probability of which depends on the size of the hash range and number of elements to be encoded. Again, false negatives aren't possible.

Let's consider a short example.

GCS example

Start with the same encrypted values 217, 354, and 466 and a hash range of decimal 128. We calculate the SHA256 hash for these values (as bytes) and then divide by the hash range to obtain a remainder between 0 and 127. This gives us the values shown in Table 10-4.

Table 10-4. GCS hash value calculation

Encrypted value	SHA256 hash of encrypted value (hex)	Hash value range 0–127
217	16badfc6202cb3f8889e0f2779b19218af4cbb736e56acadce8148aba9a7a9f8	120
354	09a1b036b82baba3177d83c27c1f7d0beacaac6de1c5fdcc9680c49f638c5fb9	57
466	826e27285307a923759de350de081d6218a04f4cff82b20c5ddaa8c60138c066	102

Sorting the reduced-range hash values into ascending order we have 57, 102, and 120. The delta values are therefore 57 (57–0), 45 (102–57), and 18 (120–102).

Our divisor power we calculate as:

$$avg = \frac{120 + 1}{3} \approx 40.33$$

$$prob = \frac{1}{40.33} \approx 0.02479$$

$$GCS\_divisor\_power\_of\_2 = \max(0, round(-log_2(-log_2(1.0 - 0.02479))) = 5$$

Using a divisor parameter of 32 (2^5), we can encode these values as shown in Table 10-5.

Table 10-5. GCS binary and unary encoding

Delta hash value range 0–127	Quotient (/32)	Remainder (%32)	Remainder (binary 5 bits)	Unary quotient (R to L with 0s)	GCS encoded
57	1	25	11001	10	1100110
45	1	13	01101	10	0110110
18	0	18	10010	1	100101

Together, last to first, left to right, the set is encoded as: 10010101101101100110.

Example: Using the PSI Process

Now that we understand the basic PSI process, let's apply it to the challenge of identifying the companies present in the list published by the UK MCA and also present in the Companies House register. If we consider the MCA as the client party and Companies House as the server party, then we can examine how to find those MCA companies that are present on the Companies House register without revealing the contents of the MCA list to Companies House.

Please note that this example is for illustration purposes only.

Environment Setup

As the PSI process is computationally intensive, we will use Google Cloud to temporarily provide us with the infrastructure to run this example.

In Chapter 6, we standardized the MCA and Companies House register datasets and saved them as standardized and cleansed CSV files. In Chapter 7, we uploaded these files onto a Google Cloud Storage bucket. For the purposes of this chapter, we will imagine that these datasets are held by two separate parties.

We will transfer these files to a single data science workbench instance on GCP upon which we will run both the server and client to illustrate the intersection process. This example can be easily extended to run on two different machines to illustrate the distinct server and client roles and the separation of data.

Google Cloud setup

To begin, we select Workbench from the AI Platform menu on the Google Cloud console. To create the environment we select User-Managed Notebooks (as opposed to Managed Notebook) as this option will allow us to install the packages we need.

The first step is to select Create New. From here we can rename the notebook to a name of our choice. Under the Environment section, select the basic Python3 option, then click Create. As in Chapter 7, you can change the region and zone settings if you wish or accept the defaults. If (optionally) you select "IAM and security," you'll note that root access to the virtual machine will be granted.

Costs

Be aware that once you create a new Workbench environment, you begin to incur costs, both when the instance is running and disk space costs even when the instance is stopped. By default the Workbench instance creates 2 × 100 GB disks!

It is your responsibility to ensure that the instance is stopped and/or deleted to avoid incurring unexpected costs.

Once your instance is created, you'll be able to click Open JupyterLab to open a local window to a JupyterLab environment hosted on your new GCP Workbench.[2] From here, we can select Terminal under Other to open a terminal window to configure our environment.

The PSI package we are going to use is released and distributed by the OpenMined community.

 OpenMined

OpenMined is an open source community whose goal is to make the world more privacy preserving by lowering the barrier-to-entry to private AI technologies. Their PSI repository provides a Private Set Intersection Cardinality protocol based on ECDH and Bloom filters.

At the time of writing, the OpenMined PSI package is available online (*https://oreil.ly/ XaKJs*). From this site we can download a prebuilt distribution compatible with a Google Cloud Workbench (currently an x86 64-bit virtual machine running Debian 11 OS) that we can readily install (option 1). Alternatively, if you prefer to use a different environment or build the package yourself, you can (option 2).

Option 1: Prebuilt PSI package

Create a PSI directory and switch into this location:

```
>>>mkdir psi
```

```
>>>cd psi
```

Copy the link address for the compatible Python distribution and use wget to download. Currently, this would be:

```
>>>wget https://files.pythonhosted.org/packages/2b/ac/
    a62c753f91139597b2baf6fb3207d29bd98a6cf01da918660c8d58a756e8/
    openmined.psi-2.0.1-cp310-cp310-manylinux_2_31_x86_64.whl
```

Install the package as follows:

```
>>>pip install openmined.psi-2.0.1-cp310-cp310-
    manylinux_2_31_x86_64.whl
```

Option 2: Build PSI package

At the terminal prompt we clone the repository for the OpenMined psi package:

```
>>>git clone http://github.com/openmined/psi
```

---

2 You may need to allow pop-ups on your local browser.

Next switch into the psi directory:

```
>>>cd psi
```

To build the psi package from the repository source we need to install the appropriate version of the build package, Bazel. Use wget to acquire the appropriate prebuilt Debian release package from the GitHub repository:

```
>>>wget https://github.com/bazelbuild/bazel/releases/download/
   6.0.0/bazel_6.0.0-linux-x86_64.deb
```

Install this package as root:

```
>>>sudo dpkg -i *.deb
```

Next we use Bazel to build the Python distribution, a wheel file, with the necessary dependencies. This step may take a few moments:

```
>>>bazel build -c opt //private_set_intersection/python:wheel
```

Once we have built the wheel archive, then we can use a Python utility provided by OpenMined to rename the file to reflect the environment it supports:

```
>>>python ./private_set_intersection/python/rename.py
```

The rename utility will output the path and name of the renamed file. We now need to install this newly renamed package from the provided path, for example:

```
>>>pip install ./bazel-bin/private_set_intersection/python/
   openmined.psi-2.0.1-cp310-cp310-manylinux_2_31_x86_64.whl
```

Again, this installation may take a few moments but once it's complete we have the building blocks we need to execute a PSI on our sample problem data.

Server install

Once our psi package is installed, one more thing we will need is a basic client/server framework to handle the matching requests. For this purpose we use the Flask lightweight microframework that we can install using pip:

```
>>>pip install flask
```

Once this install is complete, we can navigate up from the psi directory so that we can copy across our example files:

```
>>>cd ..

>>>gsutil cp gs://<your bucket>/<your path>/Chapter10* .
>>>gsutil cp gs://<your bucket>/<your path>/mari_clean.csv .
>>>gsutil cp gs://<your bucket>/<your path>/basic_clean.csv .
```

To start the flask server and run the Chapter10Server Python script, we use the following at a terminal tab prompt:

```
>>>flask --app Chapter10Server run --host 0.0.0.0
```

The server will take a few moments to start as it reads in the Companies House dataset and assembles the entities into a list of concatenated `CompanyName` and `Postcode` strings.

Once it is ready to process requests, it will display the following at the command prompt:

```
* Serving Flask app 'Chapter10Server'
...
* Running on http://127.0.0.1:5000
PRESS CTRL+C to quit
```

Server Code

Let's look at the server code by opening the Python file *Chapter10Server.py*:

```
import private_set_intersection.python as psi
from flask import Flask, request
from pandas import read_csv

fpr = 0.01
num_client_inputs = 100

df_m = read_csv('basic_clean.csv',keep_default_na=False)
server_items = ['ABLY RESOURCES G2 1PB','ADVANCE GLOBAL RECRUITMENT EH7 4HG']
#server_items = (df_m['CompanyName']+' '+ df_m['Postcode']).to_list()

app = Flask(__name__)
```

We start by importing the PSI package we installed and then the `flask` and `pandas` functions we need.

Next, we set the desired false positive rate (`fpr`) and the number of client inputs we will check in each request. Together these parameters are used to calculate the length of the Bloom filter and hash range used in GCS encoding.

We then read in the cleansed Companies House records that we transferred from our Cloud Storage bucket earlier, specifying that we ignore null values. We then create a list of server items by concatenating each of the `CompanyName` and `Postcode` values together, separated by a space. This allows us to check for an exact name and postcode match per entity.

To allow us to examine the encoding protocols in detail using a more manageable server set, I've selected two entities from the MCA list and manually created their cleansed name and postcode strings as an alternative set of server items. *To use the full Companies House dataset instead, just remove the comment marker (leading #) from the list creation statement to override the* `server_items`:

```
#server_items = (df_m['CompanyName']+' '+ df_m['Postcode']).to_list()
```

The remainder of the server file defines a class to hold the server key and then creates the key object:

```
class psikey(object):
    def __init__(self):
        self.key = None
    def set_key(self, newkey):
        self.key = newkey
        return self.key
    def get_key(self):
        return self.key


pkey = psikey()
```

The Flask web application allows us to respond to both GET and POST requests.

The server responds to a POST request to the /match path by creating a new server key and a psirequest object. We then parse the data within the POST request, process (i.e., encrypt) the received data using the new key and then serialize these processed values before returning them to the client:

```
@app.route('/match', methods=['POST'])
def match():
    s = pkey.set_key(psi.server.CreateWithNewKey(True))
    psirequest = psi.Request()
    psirequest.ParseFromString(request.data)
    return s.ProcessRequest(psirequest).SerializeToString()
```

After a match request has been processed, the server can then respond to client GET requests for the different encoding schemes: raw encrypted values, Bloom filter, and GCS. In each case, we reuse the key created during the match request and we supply the desired false positive rate and number of items in each client request so that we can configure the Bloom and GCS options:

```
@app.route('/gcssetup', methods=['GET'])
def gcssetup():
    s = pkey.get_key()
    return s.CreateSetupMessage(fpr, num_client_inputs, server_items,
        psi.DataStructure.GCS).SerializeToString()


@app.route('/rawsetup', methods=['GET'])
def rawsetup():
    s = pkey.get_key()
    return s.CreateSetupMessage(fpr, num_client_inputs, server_items,
        psi.DataStructure.RAW).SerializeToString()


@app.route('/bloomsetup', methods=['GET'])
def bloomsetup():
    s = pkey.get_key()
    return s.CreateSetupMessage(fpr, num_client_inputs, server_items,
        psi.DataStructure.BLOOM_FILTER).SerializeToString()
```

Client Code

The notebook containing the client code is *Chapter10Client.ipynb*, beginning:

```
import requests
import private_set_intersection.python as psi
from pandas import read_csv

url="http://localhost:5000/"
```

As with the server setup, we read in the cleansed MCA company details, create a client key, encrypt, and then serialize for transmission to the server.

```
df_m = read_csv('mari_clean.csv')
client_items = (df_m['CompanyName']+' '+df_m['Postcode']).to_list()
c = psi.client.CreateWithNewKey(True)
psirequest = c.CreateRequest(client_items).SerializeToString()

c.CreateRequest(client_items)
```

Prior to serialization, the first few lines of the `psirequest` look like:

```
reveal_intersection: true
encrypted_elements:
    "\002r\022JjD\303\210*\354\027\267aRId\2522\213\304\250%\005J\224\222m\354\
    207`\2136\306"
encrypted_elements:
    "\002\005\352\245r\343n\325\277\026\026\355V\007P\260\313b\377\016\000{\336\
    343\033&\217o\210\263\255[\350"
```

We include the serialized encrypted values as message content in a POST request to the /match URL path, indicating in the header that the content we are passing is a protobuf structure. The server response, containing the server-encrypted versions of the client encrypted values, is then parsed into a `response` object:

```
response = requests.post(url+'match',
    headers={'Content-Type': 'application/protobuf'}, data=psirequest)
psiresponse = psi.Response()
psiresponse.ParseFromString(response.content)
psiresponse
```

Using raw encrypted server values

To retrieve the raw encrypted server values, the client sends a request to the /raw setup URL path:

```
setupresponse = requests.get(url+'rawsetup')
rawsetup = psi.ServerSetup()
rawsetup.ParseFromString(setupresponse.content)
rawsetup
```

If we have selected to use just the two test entries in the server setup file, then we can expect only two encrypted elements in the setup response. The values will depend on the server key, but the structure will look something like this:

```
raw {
  encrypted_elements:
      "\003>W.x+\354\310\246\302z\341\364%\255\202\354\021n\t\211\037\221\255\
      263\006\305NU\345.\243@"
  encrypted_elements:
      "\003\304Q\373\224.\0348\025\3452\323\024\317l~\220\020\311A\257\002\
      014J0?\274$\031`N\035\277"
}
```

We can then calculate the intersection from the server values in the `rawsetup` structure and the `client` values in the `psiresponse` structure:

```
intersection = c.GetIntersection(gcssetup, psiresponse)
#intersection = c.GetIntersection(bloomsetup, psiresponse)
#intersection = c.GetIntersection(rawsetup, psiresponse)

iset = set(intersection)
sorted(intersection)
```

This gives us the list index of the matching entities, in this simple case:

```
[1, 2]
```

We can then look up the corresponding client entities:

```
for index in sorted(intersection):
    print(client_items[index])

ABLY RESOURCES G2 1PB
ADVANCE GLOBAL RECRUITMENT EH7 4HG
```

Success! We have resolved these entities between the client and server records, exact-matching `CompanyName` and `Postcode` attributes, without revealing the client items to the server.

Using Bloom filter–encoded encrypted server values

Now let's examine how we would use a Bloom filter to encode the set of server encrypted values:

```
setupresponse = requests.get(url+'bloomsetup')
bloomsetup = psi.ServerSetup()
bloomsetup.ParseFromString(setupresponse.content)
bloomsetup
```

If we submit a request via the /bloomsetup path, we get an output that looks like:

```
bloom_filter {
  num_hash_functions: 14
  bits: "\000\000\000\000 ...\000"
}
```

The server calculates the number of bits in the filter according to the formula in the Bloom filters section. We can re-create this as:

```python
from math import ceil, log, log2

fpr = 0.01
num_client_inputs = 10

correctedfpr = fpr / num_client_inputs
len_server_items = 2

max_elements = max(num_client_inputs, len_server_items)
num_bits = (ceil(-max_elements * log2(correctedfpr) / log(2) /8))* 8
```

The false positive rate is set at 1 in 100 per query with a batch size of 100 client items to check at a time, giving an overall (corrected) fpr of 0.0001. For our very basic example, max_elements is also equal to 100. This gives us a Bloom filter bit length of 1920:

```python
num_hash_functions = ceil(-log2(correctedfpr))
```

This gives us 14 hash functions.

We can reproduce the Bloom filter by processing the raw encrypted server elements:

```python
from hashlib import sha256

#num_bits = len(bloomsetup.bloom_filter.bits)*8
filterlist = ['0'] * num_bits
for element in rawsetup.raw.encrypted_elements:
    element1 = str.encode('1') + element
    k = sha256(element1).hexdigest()
    h1 = int(k,16) % num_bits

    element2 = str.encode('2') + element
    k = sha256(element2).hexdigest()
    h2 = int(k,16) % num_bits

    for i in range(bloomsetup.bloom_filter.num_hash_functions):
        pos = ((h1 + i * h2) % num_bits)
        filterlist[num_bits-1-pos]='1'

filterstring = ''.join(filterlist)
```

Then we can compare our filter against the filter bits returned by the server when assembled in the same order and converted to a string:

```
bloombits = ''.join(format(byte, '08b') for byte in
    reversed(bloomsetup.bloom_filter.bits))
bloombits == filterstring
```

Using GCS-encoded encrypted server values

Finally, let's examine how we would use GCS to encode the set of server-encrypted values.

```
setupresponse = requests.get(url+'gcssetup')
gcssetup =
    psi.ServerSetup()gcssetup.ParseFromString(setupresponse.content)
```

If we submit a request via the /gcssetup path, we get an output that looks like:

```
gcs {
  div: 17
  hash_range: 1000000
  bits: ")![Q\026"
}
```

To reproduce these values, we can apply the formulas in the preceding PSI section:

```
from math import ceil, log, log2

fpr = 0.01
num_client_inputs = 100
correctedfpr = fpr/num_client_inputs

hash_range = max_elements/correctedfpr
hash_range
```

This gives us the hash range of 1000000.

As with Bloom filter, we can reproduce the GCS structure by processing the raw encrypted server elements. First, we hash the raw encrypted server values into the gcs_hash_range, sort in ascending order, and calculate the differences:

```
from hashlib import sha256

ulist = []
for element in rawsetup.raw.encrypted_elements:
    k = sha256(element).hexdigest()
    ks = int(k,16) % gcssetup.gcs.hash_range
    ulist.append(ks)

ulist.sort()
udiff = [ulist[0]] + [ulist[n]-ulist[n-1]
    for n in range(1,len(ulist))]
```

Now we can calculate the GCS divisor as:

```
avg = (ulist[-1]+1)/len(ulist)
prob = 1/avg
gcsdiv = max(0,round(-log2(-log2(1.0-prob))))
```

This gives us a divisor of 17, which we can then use to calculate the quotient and remainder before we encode these in unary and binary, respectively. We concatenate these bit patterns together:

```
encoded = ''
for diff in udiff:
    if diff != 0:
        quot = int(diff / pow(2,gcssetup.gcs.div))
        rem = diff % pow(2,gcssetup.gcs.div)

        next = '{0:b}'.format(rem) + '1' + ('0' * quot)
        pad = next.zfill(quot+gcssetup.gcs.div+1)
        encoded = pad + encoded
```

Finally, we pad out the encoded string to be a multiple of 8 so that we can match against the returned GCS bits:

```
from math import ceil
padlength = ceil(len(encoded)/8)*8
padded = encoded.zfill(padlength)

gcsbits = ''.join(format(byte, '08b') for byte in
    reversed(gcssetup.gcs.bits))
gcsbits == padded
```

Full MCA and Companies House Sample Example

Now that we have seen the end-to-end PSI entity matching process using a tiny server dataset of only two items, we're ready to use the full Companies House dataset.

Open the *Chapter10Server.py* file and uncomment:

```
#server_items = (df_m['CompanyName']+' '+
    df_m['Postcode']).to_list()
```

and then stop (Ctrl+C or Cmd-C) and restart the Flask server:

```
>>>flask --app Chapter10Server run --host 0.0.0.0
```

Now we can restart the client kernel and rerun the notebook to get the full intersection between the MCA and Companies House data, resolving the entities on CompanyName and Postcode.

We can request either a raw, Bloom, or GCS response. Allow approximately 10 minutes for the server to process and return. *I suggest you skip over the steps to reproduce the Bloom/GCS structures as these could take quite a while.*

Jumping to calculate the intersection then gives us 45 exact matches:

```
ADVANCE GLOBAL RECRUITMENT EH7 4HG
ADVANCED RESOURCE MANAGERS PO6 4PR
...

WORLDWIDE RECRUITMENT SOLUTIONS WA15 8AB
```

 Tidy Up

Remember to stop and delete your User-Managed Notebook and any associated disks to avoid ongoing charges!

This PSI example has shown how we can resolve entities between two parties even if one party cannot share their data with the other. In this basic example, we have been able to look for simultaneous exact matches on only two attributes.

In certain situations, exact matching may be sufficient. However, when approximate matching is needed, and at least one party is prepared to share partial matches, we need a more sophisticated approach that is beyond the scope of this book. There is ongoing research into the practicality of using fully homomorphic encryption to enable privacy-preserving fuzzy matching, which would open up a wider field of potential use cases for this technique.[3]

Summary

In this chapter we learned how to use Private Set Intersection to resolve entities between two parties without either party revealing their full dataset. We saw how to use compressed data representations to reduce the volume of data we needed to pass between the two parties at the price of introducing a small percentage of false positives.

We noted that these techniques can be readily applied to exact matching scenarios but that more advanced approximate or probabilistic matching remains a challenge and a subject of active research.

---

3 See the patent "Compact fuzzy private matching using a fully-homomorphic encryption scheme," *https://patents.google.com/patent/US20160119119*.

CHAPTER 11

Further Considerations

Hopefully the previous chapters have given you a solid practical understanding of how to resolve entities within your datasets and have equipped you to overcome some of the challenges you are likely to meet along the way.

Real-world data is messy and full of surprises, so joining it up is rarely straightforward. But it's well worth spending the time to make the connections because the story becomes so much richer when we can bring together all the pieces of the jigsaw.

In this short closing chapter, I'll talk about a few aspects of entity resolution that are worth considering when building a resilient production solution. I'll also share some closing thoughts on the future of the art and science of entity resolution.

Data Considerations

As with any analytic process, the importance of understanding the context and quality of your input data cannot be overstated. Quirks or misunderstandings in data that a traditional application could tolerate may fundamentally derail a matching process. Poor data can result in over- and underlinking, sometimes matching entities that do not represent the same person, with potentially serious consequences.

In this section, I'll discuss the most important data-related issues to consider when performing entity resolution.

Unstructured Data

Throughout this book we have primarily used structured data to perform the matching process. When we encountered semi-unstructured data we used very simple rules of thumb to extract the attributes we needed. For example, in Chapter 2, we somewhat arbitrarily split full name strings into `Firstname` and `Lastname`, and in

Chapter 6, we extracted only the postcode from the full address text. In the name of simplicity, we neglected potentially valuable data that could have enriched our matching process.

Fortunately, the state of the art in extracting meaning from unstructured text has developed considerably in the last few years. Advances in named entity recognition (NER) techniques for understanding sentence construction, and extracting entities in context, mean we can more easily link to unstructured content.

For example, there are several Python libraries available (such as usaddress, deepparse, and libpostal) that can parse addresses, extracting individual house number, street, and town attributes. The performance of these models depends on the availability of high-quality training data and so varies by country.

However, even the most sophisticated NER cannot make up for the absence of key attributes if they are not present in the source text. News articles, for example, will rarely provide a date of birth for their subjects, and financial transactions will not typically include a social security number.

Data Quality

In our illustrative examples, we have accepted much of our input data at face value and taken expedient shortcuts to prepare our data for matching. For example, as a shortcut, we simply dropped records that contained an attribute with a missing value. Our process should be able to ignore (i.e., assign a zero match weight to that attribute) as opposed to discarding the whole record. For a production solution, a more rigorous approach to measuring and continuously improving data quality is vital. The better the data quality, the easier the matching task will be.

Additional data checks for completeness and validity (including identifying hidden and unexpected characters) will alert you to problems that may frustrate your matching process in unexpected ways and are challenging to diagnose further down the line.

Temporal Equivalence

The entity resolution process relies on matching attributes to determine whether records refer to the same real-world entity. However, the attributes associated with an entity may change over time. Last names may change with marital status; phone numbers and email addresses may change as individuals swap service providers; passports, driving licenses, and other forms of identification are reissued with new identifiers.

It sounds obvious, but this temporal aspect of entity resolution is often overlooked, so my advice is to be careful with datasets that contain data drawn from different time periods and ensure the model doesn't place too much weight on attributes that are subject to change. Of course, where the entity is trying not to be identified, frequent attribute changes can be sign of a deliberate attempt to frustrate the entity resolution process.

Attribute Comparison

In Chapter 3, we explored some of the most commonly used techniques for approximate string matching. We considered edit distance and phonetic equivalence to determine a match between discrete name attributes. These approaches work well when we have a single token, such as a discrete element of a name, to compare. When we are faced with assessing the similarity between two strings with multiple words or tokens, such as addresses or the names of organizations, then there are other techniques we can consider.

Set Matching

When an entity is identified by a collection of terms, we can use set-based methods (such as Jaccard index[1]) to measure the degree of overlap between the tokens present in each set. More sophisticated methods, such as Monge-Elkan similarity, combine both set-based and edit distance techniques to perform the comparison.

Recent advances in sentence embedding[2] now allow us to translate the semantic meaning of a string of text into a vector (an array of quantities in number of dimensions). These vectorizing models, trained on vast repositories of open source data, are accessible through public interfaces, such as OpenAI's embedding API. The semantic similarity of these text strings can then be assessed by techniques such as cosine similarity, which measures the angle between the vectors.

Vector-based approaches can also be applied to measure the similarity between individual words (represented as strings of single characters or multiple character n-grams) but they typically do not consider the sequence of these letters, which can be extremely important in matching, e.g., NAB (an Australian bank) versus NBA (a US basketball organization).

Geocoding Location Matching

An alternative to matching the individual words, or tokens, that comprise an address is to convert the address into a set of geographic coordinates (latitude and longitude). We can then compare these values within a set straight line distance tolerance to determine if they refer to the same place. Clearly, for multioccupancy locations in

---

1 For more details on the Jaccard index, visit the Wikipedia page (*https://oreil.ly/vJyir*).

2 Further details on how to use the sent2vec library are available in the PyPI documentation (*https://oreil.ly/SUHrG*).

close proximity (within a shared building or industrial estate, for example), this approach can produce a number of false positives.

At the time of writing Google, Microsoft, and OpenStreetMap (via Nominatim) offer geocoding APIs that will perform the conversion, subject to pricing and usage policies. As an on-demand software as a service (SaaSso) offering, this approach may not be suitable for bulk address comparison or where the data is sensitive and cannot be shared with third parties.

Aggregating Comparisons

As we have seen, there are often several different techniques we can use to compare attributes, each with their strengths and weaknesses. In certain use cases it may be beneficial to evaluate a potential match using multiple approaches, for example, using both a Soundex comparison and an edit distance measurement to determine the most appropriate result.

It should be noted that if parallel techniques are used on the same attributes, then the results will not respect the conditional independence assumption of the Fellegi-Sunter model and therefore may not perform well when using probabilistic tools such as Splink. In particular, the different measurements should be included at different comparison levels within a single comparison to avoid double counting. Alternatively, these different measurements could be preaggregated into a single score using a custom similarity function.

Post Processing

In Chapter 10, we saw how we can group paired records into a single distinct cluster. We also introduced the challenge of determining which attribute values to use to describe our unified entity. The selection logic to choose which attribute value to promote is likely to be bespoke to your use case and may depend upon the relative trustworthiness and seniority of your datasets.

Once a canonical entity view has been established, there is the opportunity to repeat the pairwise matching exercise, treating the newly consolidated entity as a new record. Additional records, previously too dissimilar to match, may now reach the equivalence threshold due to the concentration of attributes in the new composite entity.

For example, consider the input records shown in Table 11-1. Records 1 and 2 may be assessed as referring to the same individual (based on equivalent first name and date of birth) but Record 3 does not have sufficient commonality with either to join that small cluster.

Table 11-1. Entity resolution—input

Attribute	Record 1	Record 2	Record 3
First name	Michael	Michael	M
Last name	Shearer	Shear	Shearer
Date of birth	4/1/1970	4/1/1970	
Place of birth		Stow on the Wold	Stow on the Wold
Mobile number			07700 900999

Having resolved Records 1 and 2 into a single entity, suppose we choose the value "Shearer" over "Shear" to represent the last name. Perhaps Record 1 was part of a dataset that was deemed of higher quality than that containing Record 2. Or perhaps we implemented a rule to select the more complete value. As shown in Table 11-2, we would then have a richer set of attributes to match against Record 3.

Table 11-2. Entity resolution—pairwise clustering

Attribute	Cluster 1 Record 1 and 2	Record 3
First name	Michael	M
Last name	Shearer	Shearer
Date of birth	4/1/1970	
Place of birth	Stow on the Wold	Stow on the Wold
Mobile number		07700 900999

If an exact last name match and equivalent place of birth were deemed sufficient evidence, then we could conclude that Record 3 should now join the cluster of Records 1 and 2.

As shown in Table 11-3, we have now resolved all three records into a single entity and, thanks to our additional step, added a phone number that we would otherwise not have linked to our entity.

Table 11-3. Entity resolution—entity record resolution

Attribute	Cluster 1 Record 1, 2, and 3
First name	Michael
Last name	Shearer
Date of birth	4/1/1970
Place of birth	Stow on the Wold
Mobile number	07700 900999

This shows how we can progressively build the confidence to join these records into a single clustered entity. This is an example of "bottom up," or agglomerative hierarchical clustering. In this simple example, we exhaustively linked all three records, but in larger datasets there would have been many more candidates to compare and potentially cluster together in subsequent iterations.

In Chapter 8, we saw how the Google Cloud Entity Reconciliation service uses this technique. The Google service specifies a number of iterations after which it terminates the clustering process. Clearly, this approach can be computationally intensive on large datasets and is not guaranteed to find the optimum solution.

Graphical Representation

After attribute comparison and pairwise match classification, the final steps in the entity resolution process overlap quite significantly with the field of graph analytics.

As we saw in Chapter 10, the output of the clustering process can be presented as an entity graph of source records (nodes) and a set of matching attribute pairs (edges). This representation may form part of a wider network graph showing how distinct entities are connected via shared relationships or common attributes. This representation is useful to allow inspection (and potential discounting) of the matches informed by the context of their wider network.

Alternatively, if matching confidence is high, or a simpler representation is required, the entity graph can resolve (or collapse) to a single node. That node can either list a canonical set of attributes or persist the alternative attribute values for closer examination. This curated network, or knowledge graph, provides a combined view of all the information about a given entity drawn from different sources.

You may have noticed that this is partly how Google search works today. Search results now present factual information from Google's Knowledge Graph (*https://oreil.ly/H59UU*), which contains over 500 million objects with over 3.5 billion facts about, and relationships between, these different objects. As we saw in Chapter 8, you can now resolve your entities against Google's objects using their reconciliation API.

Real-Time Considerations

In this book, we have considered batch-based entity resolution of static datasets. This point-in-time approach allows us to compare, match, and cluster all relevant records to produce a set of resolved entities. This reference point can then be used for a period of time before becoming stale and the exercise repeated. In Chapter 6, we saw how to pairwise match a new record against an existing dataset using a pretrained probabilistic model.

If an up-to-the-minute set of all resolved entities is required, then incrementally processing new records as they arrive brings with it some additional considerations. Depending upon the processing time window available, it may be challenging to recluster and generate new canonical entities based on the contents of a newly available record, or to reshape existing entities into a new configuration.

Performance Evaluation

The functional performance of an entity resolution solution may be evaluated by the extent to which records are matched when then they are truly distinct (overlinking) or remain unconnected when they refer to the same real-world entity (underlinking). The nature of the decisions and actions you propose to take based on the resolved dataset will determine the relative priority of these metrics. For example, in a high-risk situation, where the consequence of missing a link could be significant, you may wish to err toward overlinking. In a more speculative process, you may wish to lean toward underlinking to minimize unnecessary customer friction.

Systematic evaluation of the degree to which your solution is over- or underlinking is challenging. In the earlier chapters of this book, we had the benefit of a known population against which we could evaluate the precision, recall, and accuracy of our process. But in practice that is rarely the case. The need to resolve entities usually arises as a result of the lack of a common key or known population between datasets, thereby depriving the evaluator of ground truth against which to measure performance.

Smaller benchmark datasets, which can be affordably manually linked, are often used to predict performance at scale. However, these limited datasets can give a distorted view of the likely real-world outcomes. Larger datasets are more likely to contain distinct entities that have similar attributes (e.g., same name), increasing the rate of false positives. Care must also be taken to make sure the distribution of benchmark dataset is accounted for in the evaluation process. The ratio of matching to nonmatching records is often significantly higher in benchmark datasets that are constructed to check that the matching process finds the right matches (i.e., maximizes recall) but gives an overly optimistic view of the frequency of errors (i.e., overestimates precision). There is also a risk, particularly for the more sophisticated embedding-based approaches, of overfitting the entity resolution model because the benchmark data was represented in the training data, resulting in poor generalized performance.

Evaluating the performance of an entity resolution solution is a critical part of model development and improvement. It requires labeling data that can then be used to train more sophisticated models or to estimate performance metrics such as precision and recall.

There are two main approach types to data labeling and performance evaluation in entity resolution applications:

Pairwise approach
    Labeling a set of record pairs as a match and not a match

Cluster-based approach
    Identifying or using a set of known, fully resolved entities (clusters)

Pairwise Approach

Using a pairwise approach we can estimate precision, i.e., how often we are correct when we declare a match, by simply sampling pairs of matched records and manually reviewing them. Once classified as true or false positives, we can calculate precision as:

$$Precision = \frac{True\ positives}{(True\ positives + False\ positives)}$$

To estimate recall is more challenging, as we essentially have to repeat the resolution exercise to identify records that should have been declared a match but were not. This can be more efficiently estimated by selecting a block of loosely matching records and then exhaustively reviewing all the potential pairs of records within this block. Of course, as with any blocking approach, we risk overlooking wildcard matches that didn't make it into our loosely selected block.

As a reminder, recall is calculated as:

$$Recall = \frac{True\ positives}{(True\ positives + False\ negatives)}$$

Cluster-Based Approach

An alternative to the pairwise approach is to manually determine, for example, through the use of search tools, a true cluster view of those records that described the same real-world entity. We can then compare our pairwise predictions against this gold standard to assess our performance and improve our model. For example, consider the simple example shown in Figure 11-1.

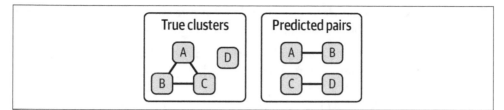

Figure 11-1. Cluster-based evaluation example

Within a population of four records, A to D, our model has paired records A + B and C + D. A true cluster view shows that A, B, and C all refer to the same entity but D is distinct. From this, we can assess the following and calculate our performance metrics.

Record pair	Predicted	Actual	Result
A - B	Match	Match	True positive
A - C	Not match	Match	False negative
A - D	Not match	Not match	True negative
B - C	Not match	Match	False negative
B - D	Not match	Not match	True negative
C - D	Match	Not match	False positive

The evaluation of entity resolution is an area of active research with toolsets emerging to assist with the process and produce actionable feedback to improve performance.[3]

Future of Entity Resolution

Entity resolution is by definition a means to an end. By resolving entities, we seek to assemble all the relevant information from multiple sources to enable us to derive valuable insights and ultimately make better decisions.

In an increasingly digital world, we have a shared responsibility to ensure that our data records accurately and comprehensively reflect society. If we have incorrect information, or only part of the picture, we risk drawing the wrong conclusions and taking the wrong actions. There is also a duty to respect individual privacy and to manage sensitive data accordingly.

The art and science of entity resolution is evolving to balance these concerns. Entity resolution can enhance your ability to connect the dots in your data and show the bigger picture. Increasingly it can be done without unnecessarily sharing personal

---

3 For example, an open source Python package for the evaluation of entity resolution (ER) systems is available on GitHub (*https://github.com/Valires/er-evaluation*).

information. New machine learning algorithms, and techniques to more rigorously evaluate and optimize their performance, are now freely available.

Recent advancements in the scale and availability of large language models (LLMs) open up a breadth of information about how real-world entities are described and interrelated. The embedding technology that underpins these models provides a rich context to inform the matching processes. The increasing availability of managed entity resolution services and the ability to relate your entities to public knowledge repositories promises to make the matching process easier and the results richer.

I hope you have enjoyed our shared journey through the challenges of entity resolution and that you feel ready to join the dots in your data. Who knows what you will find...

Index

Metaphone algorithm, 33
middle initials, 25
mismatches, resolving, 23-26
misspelling errors, 4-5, 31
MRA (Match Rating Approach), 34

N

naive Bayes, 49
naive PSI, 149
name matching, 1
named entity recognition (NER), 168
names, checking for spaces in, 21
naming conventions, standardizing, 43
NetworkX, 94
new entities, matching, 87
nodes, 89, 172

O

OpenMined PSI package, 157
outer joins, 23

P

package managers, 15, 30
pairwise comparisons, 89-90, 92, 93-95,
    105-109 (see also clustering)
pairwise evaluation, 174
pandas DataFrames
    appending additional columns to, 64
    cross-product dataset, 82
    normalizing JSON prior to concatenation,
        65
    outer joins, 23
    removing blank rows, 20
    selecting TheyWorkForYou data, 18-19
    selecting Wikipedia data, 17
    standardizing column names, 21, 80
    transposing columns, 80
performance, measuring
    cloud entity resolution services, 144
    cluster-based approach, 174
    company matching, 85-87
    data standardization, 26
    functional performance, 173
    pairwise approach, 174
    recall and precision, 10
    record blocking, 75
    Spark and Google Cloud Platform, 126
    systematic evaluation, 173

text matching, 39
performance, predicting, 173
phonetic matching, 30, 33
pip package manager, 15, 30
post processing, 170-172
postcodes, 81
precision, 10, 26, 39
privacy considerations
    cryptographic hash functions, 149
    how PSI (private set intersection) works,
        148
    naive PSI, 149
    OpenMined PSI package, 157
    privacy preserving record linkage, 147
    PSI process example, 155-166
    PSI protocol based on ECDH, 150-155
    PSI technique, 147
    PSI use cases, 148
probabilistic matching
    benefits of, 41
    expectation-maximization (EM) algorithm,
        51-56
    models for, 47-51
    multiple attribute match probability, 45
    privacy challenges, 166
    single attribute match probability, 43-45
Python
    address parsing libraries, 168
    Beautiful Soup package, 16, 19, 65
    client to handle reconciliation jobs, 142-144
    downloading and installing, 14
    Jellyfish package, 30
    kernel configuration, 16
    kernel restarts, 30
    NetworkX package, 94
    pip package manager, 15, 30
    tutorials and further reading, xi
    virtual environment, 15

Q

questions and comments, x, xii

R

real-time versus static data, 172
recall, 10, 26, 39
reconciliation jobs, 135-140
record blocking
    attribute comparison, 67-73
    for clustering, 96-101

About the Author

Michael Shearer is Chief Solution Officer at HAWK:AI, whose mission is to help financial institutions detect financial crime. A former HSBC Managing Director, Michael led the development of a full suite of financial crime detection and investigation capabilities, including the design and deployment of award-winning dynamic risk assessment and contextual monitoring platforms. Michael also has 20 years experience in UK government service in a variety of sensitive operational and technical roles. He holds a masters in electrical and electronic engineering from Queen's University Belfast.

Colophon

The animal on the cover of *Hands-On Entity Resolution* is a coppersmith barbet (*Psilopogon haemacephalus*), also known as a crimson-breasted barbet. They are known for having a metronomic bird call that sounds similar to a coppersmith's hammer hitting metal.

Coppersmith barbets are small birds (15 to 17 centimeters long) that weigh between 1 and 2 ounces. They are predominantly green birds with a crimson head, yellow cheeks, and a yellow throat. Their underparts are streaked with gray and black.

Coppersmiths can be found on the Indian subcontinent and across parts of Southeast Asia, including but not limited to Bangladesh, Thailand, Malaysia, and Pakistan. It is essential for their habitat to have dead wood, as they use their beaks to carve their nests into the wood. They can be found in a variety of habitats, such as gardens, groves, and sparse woodlands, where they enjoy eating a variety of wild figs, drupes and berries, flower petals, and the occasional insect. They are able to eat between 1.5 and 3 times their weight in berries every day.

Populations of coppersmith barbets are on the rise, and they are considered a species of least concern on endangered species lists. However, many of the animals on O'Reilly covers are endangered; all of them are important to the world.

The cover illustration is by Karen Montgomery, based on an antique line engraving from *Lydekker's Royal Natural History*. The series design is by Edie Freedman, Ellie Volckhausen, and Karen Montgomery. The cover fonts are Gilroy Semibold and Guardian Sans. The text font is Adobe Minion Pro; the heading font is Adobe Myriad Condensed; and the code font is Dalton Maag's Ubuntu Mono.

O'REILLY®

Learn from experts.
Become one yourself.

Books | Live online courses
Instant answers | Virtual events
Videos | Interactive learning

Get started at oreilly.com.

Printed in the USA
CPSIA information can be obtained
at www.ICGtesting.com
JSHW050026090724
66058JS00007B/105

9 781098 148485